Table of Contents

WORKBOOK ON ESTATES AND FUTURE INTERESTS

By

Raymond R. Coletta
Professor of Law
University of the Pacific,
McGeorge School of Law

Mat #40358311

COPYRIGHT © 1994 WEST PUBLISHING

© West, a Thomson business, 2000, 2004

© 2005 Thomson/West

      610 Opperman Drive

      P.O. Box 64526

      St. Paul, MN 55164–0526

      1–800–328–9352

Printed in the United States of America

ISBN–13: 978–0–314–16021–8

ISBN–10: 0–314–16021–3

TEXT IS PRINTED ON 10% POST
CONSUMER RECYCLED PAPER

I. Introduction

This Workbook begins with an analysis of the grant of a fee simple estate and builds sequentially toward more complicated interests and conveyances.

The initial chapters emphasize the recognition of the basic forms of estates and future interests. Each of these chapters begins with a brief discussion of the defining characteristics and special language associated with the respective estate or future interest and then provides ten problems that illustrate how the estate or interest is expressed within the context of a given conveyance.

The later chapters deal with several general rules focused on destroying certain future interests, and thereby making land more marketable. Each of these chapters begins with a brief explanation of the particular rule and a review of its commonly defined elements. Again, this is followed by ten problems, illustrating how the particular rule may be implicated in various types of conveyances.

The Workbook is designed to proceed from simple to complex. Later problems build on the successful command of earlier material. You should attempt to gain a firm understanding of all the steps of analysis for each problem before beginning the next one. At each stage, each problem is completely analyzed so earlier concepts are constantly reviewed. As in learning any language, repetition forwards familiarity and comfort, and, ultimately, understanding.

Please note, this Workbook is not intended to be an exhaustive treatise on estates and future interests. Many specialized applications and rules are not illustrated. The goal of this Workbook is to provide a working knowledge of the area's central concepts.

How To Use This Workbook

Determining the state of title for conveyances of estates in land can be a simple process. Most of the rules governing this area are straightforward and easily understood. Difficulties often arise when students attempt to apply common meanings to a conveyance's individual words and then interpret these meanings within the context of the "whole" sentence. Because of the historical context within which conveyancing arose, the actual state of title produced may be far different than the words seem to connote. Conveyances are technical constructs and must be analyzed within specific parameters. It is crucial to realize that the legal consequences of the grant may be quite different from the common meanings that words seems to forward. Keep in mind that conveyances use a highly specialized lexicon. Be wary of slipping into a layperson's interpretation of these very specialized terms.

A key to success is to proceed slowly. Discard your propensity to "read" each conveyance and apply common English meanings to the terms. Discipline yourself to move deliberately through a two-step process of (i) translation and (ii) analysis.

Step 1. Translation (T)

In this initial step, common words and phrases are rewritten with their required, technical meanings. Both the identity of the transferee and the type of estate created are dependent on the language used in the conveyance. Certain words create certain estates regardless of their meanings under today's language usage. For example, the phrase "and his heirs" usually does not indicate a grant to the transferor's heirs; rather "and his heirs" should be translated into the phrase "in fee simple," the real meaning of the term (due to historical happenstance). You should begin your dissection of a conveyance by translating, as needed, the words of the conveyance into their technical, legal meanings.

Step 2. <u>Analysis</u> (SoT)

After mechanically translating all needed terms, you can then proceed to determine the state of title conveyed. Essentially, this consists of categorizing all interests created or retained, both in the present and the future. Rules governing the creation of interests are very straightforward. Remember, do not attempt to read the conveyance and "understand" its terminology in terms of today's common English meanings. Read the conveyance sequentially. Apply the applicable rules mechanically.

> Translate first. Mechanically apply the rules second.
>
> Read with blinders. Read sequentially. Take small, deliberate steps.

Mechanics

Estates are created through specific words that have special legal significance: words of purchase and words of limitation. **Words of purchase** are words that identify to whom the estate is transferred. **Words of limitation** are words that describe the type of estate that is being created.

In the conveyance "Ernie grants Greenacre to Bert for life then to Kermit and his heirs," the words of purchase "to Bert" and "to Ernie" denote that these individuals receive an interest and therefore are grantees of the estate. The words of limitation "for life" and "and his heirs" identify the present estate as a life estate and the future interest as a fee simple. In general, when you analyze a conveyance, the first step is to recognize the words of limitation and translate them into their proper meanings. In the boxes below the conveyances, "T" (for "translation") indicates this step. Here you should simply rewrite the conveyance by translating the words of limitation into the estates they indicate.

Ex: Ernie ➔ Bert for life and to Kermit and his heirs.

T	Ernie to Bert in life estate, then to Kermit in fee simple.

Once you have translated the words of limitation, the next step is to analyze which estates and future interests are created by the conveyance. "SoT" (for "state of title") is a listing of the interests (both present and future) that are conveyed to each party to the grant. In the above example, the current state of title (as you will soon learn) is that Bert has a life estate followed by Kermit's vested remainder in fee simple (a future interest which will become immediately possessory at the expiration of Bert's life estate). The completed conveyancing box would appear as follows:

T	Ernie to Bert in life estate, then to Kermit in fee simple.
SoT	Bert - life estate Kermit - vested remainder in fee simple

Below this box you should write a complete analysis of how the state of title was determined. This is the heart of the process. You must learn to provide a detailed analysis for each interest indicated in your state of title. Each analysis should provide a thorough explanation of which estates and future interests arise and why. This workbook contains complete answers to all problems. As you progress through the book, your own analysis should begin to reflect the detail found in these answers. Determining the correct state of title necessitates an ability to fully explain the steps taken in characterizing each interest. Remember, the ability to explain why you think a certain interest is created is more important than serendipitously arriving at the correct categorization.

Glossary

Afterborn – a child conceived before, but born after, the death of the grantor. An afterborn child is considered to be alive from the time of conception, if such a fiction would benefit the child's interests. For the purposes of the Rule Against Perpetuities, a child conceived, but not yet born, at the time of conveyance is considered a life in being.

Alternative Contingent Remainders – contingent remainders created in the same conveyance, each dependent on the same condition for vesting. If one contingent remainder vests, the other cannot. A contingent remainder followed by a "but if" clause often will be followed by an alternative contingent remainder. When the grantor creates alternative contingent remainders, the grantor retains a reversion.

Ascertainable Individual – an individual (or defined group) whose identity is certain and who is in existence at the time of conveyance. If, at the time of conveyance, the grantor has one son, then "to my only son" describes an individual whose identity is certain and who is in existence at the time of conveyance. Generally, an ascertainable individual is someone to whom the grantor can point. Individuals who are not certain, or do not exist at the time of conveyance, are unascertainable.

Condition - a set of facts which must be met for an estate or interest to vest, continue, or end.

Condition Precedent – a condition that must be met before a future interest will vest. See: Remainders.

Contingent Remainder - a contingent remainder is a remainder that is (i) subject to a condition precedent, or (ii) held by an unascertainable person. A reversion will always follow a contingent remainder (so that someone will hold seisin if the interest fails to vest).

Cy Pres – "as near as possible". When a conveyance violates the Rule Against Perpetuities, some jurisdictions allow the court to alter the conveyance so that it no longer exceeds the perpetuities period. This alteration must be consistent with the general intent of the grantor. Some jurisdictions apply Cy Pres to interests which have not vested by the end of a wait-and-see period.

Destructibility of Contingent Remainders, Doctrine of – a doctrine that makes land more marketable by destroying contingent remainders. In a destructibility jurisdiction, a remainder is destroyed if it doesn't vest at, or before, the termination of the previous estate. The remainder is extinguished forever, and seisin moves on to the next vested estate. In a non-destructibility jurisdiction, seisin reverts back to the grantor (usually as a fee simple on executory limitation) until the remainder can vest. See: Rules furthering Marketability.

Divest – to "cut short" or terminate an estate before its natural duration. Thus, a life estate is divested (cut short) if it ends before the death of the measuring life. Because a fee simple has potentially limitless duration, the termination of a fee simple estate is always a divestment.

Equitable Interest (or Estate) – an interest held by virtue of equitable title or on equitable grounds. The holder of an equitable interest often does not have legal title to property, but does have certain enforceable equitable rights (for example the right to income from the property). The beneficiary of a trust has an equitable interest in the property managed by the trust, while the trustee has a legal interest in the property and holds legal title.

Executory Interest – one of two types of future interests created in a transferee. An executory interest is a future interest that divests the preceding estate upon the satisfaction of a condition. A shifting executory interest divests a transferee. A springing executory interest divests the transferor. Executory interests are alienable, devisable, and inheritable.

Fee Simple – The largest quantum estate, consisting of a right to total ownership both in the present and in perpetuity. A fee simple is fully alienable, devisable, and inheritable. Because fee simple interests are fully marketable, they are highly favored; ambiguities regarding the type of estate created are generally resolved in favor of finding a fee simple estate.

Fee Simple Absolute – a fee simple interest, specifically a fee simple interest which is not defeasible.

Fee Simple Defeasible – a fee simple which may end upon the occurrence of a stated future event. Fee Simple Defeasibles consist of the fee simple determinable, fee simple subject to condition subsequent, and fee simple on executory limitation.

Fee Simple Determinable – a fee simple estate which will automatically revert to the grantor when a certain condition occurs or fails to occur. The conveyance's wording usually contains words of duration introducing the condition that divests the estate: "as long as," "while," "until," and "during." This estate is alienable, devisable, and inheritable. When a fee simple determinable is created, the grantor retains a future interest (representing the right to repossess) known as a possibility of reverter. See: Fee Simple on Executory Limitation, Possibility of Reverter.

Fee Simple Subject to Condition Subsequent – a fee simple estate which may be terminated at the grantor's election when a certain condition occurs or fails to occur. The conveyance usually contains words introducing the condition that divests the grantee of the estate: "provided that," "but if," and "on condition that." Modernly, in most jurisdictions, where the type of defeasible fee is ambiguous, a fee simple subject to condition subsequent is presumed. This estate is alienable, devisable, and inheritable. When a Fee Simple Subject to Condition Subsequent is created, the grantor retains a future interest (representing the right to elect to repossess) known as a right of entry. See: Fee simple on Executory Limitation, Right of Entry.

Fee Simple on Executory Limitation – a fee simple defeasible estate where the right to repossess (upon the occurrence of the condition) is created in a third party, rather than in the grantor. Whenever the right to repossess is created in a third party, regardless of whether repossession is automatic or by election, the estate created is a fee simple on executory limitation. The future interest held by the third party is always an executory interest, regardless of whether it becomes possessory automatically or by election. The Fee Simple on Executory Limitation is alienable, devisable, and inheritable.

Fee Tail – an estate which provides the transferee and the transferee's direct lineal descendants present possession so long as the transferee's bloodline continues. The transferor retains a future interest known as a reversion, which becomes possessory should the transferee's bloodline fail. The holder of the present possessory interest may only alienate the right to possession during the holder's life. This interest is not devisable. It is inheritable only by lineal descendants in the manner described in the fee tail grant. See: Reversion.

Future Interest – an interest in an estate which is not yet possessory, but which may become possessory at some time in the future. The holder of a future interest does not have traditional possessory property rights such as the right to possess, occupy, or exclude, but does have a protected interest in future possession of the property. See: Waste, Doctrine of.

Heirs – a person who is entitled to receive property upon the death of an individual. A living individual has no heirs, only "heirs apparent." Conveyances to an individual's heirs are somewhat problematic, since these individuals are only ascertainable at the individual's death. See: Words of Limitation, Words of Purchase.

Heirs Apparent – while alive, an individual does not have any heirs, only heirs apparent. Heirs apparent are those individuals who, at that point in time, are likely to become heirs upon the individual's death.

Inter Vivos Transfer – a transfer of a real property interest made during life. See: Testamentary transfer.

Laches, Doctrine of – a doctrine applicable in various jurisdictions that requires an interest or right to be asserted within a certain amount of time, or else it is extinguished.

Legal Interest (or Estate) – the holder of a legal interest has record title to, and ownership of, that interest. A trustee who holds title to property has legal title to that property. The trust beneficiary, while holding no title to property, has an equitable interest in the property. See: Equitable Interest (or Estate), Trust, transfers in.

Life Estate – an estate whose duration is measured by a particular human life. A life estate is alienable, but because it terminates on the death of the individual, it is neither devisable nor inheritable.

Life Estate per autre vie – a life estate held by one individual which is measured by the life of another. Per autre vie is Latin meaning "during the life of another." If a life estate is alienated, the new owner receives a life estate measured by the original owner's life. A life estate per autre vie is alienable, inheritable, and devisable; but, like the original life estate, ends upon the death of the original measuring life.

Marketability – marketability refers to the ability of certain interests in land to be transferred on the open market. Estates which are fragmented between present and unascertainable future interest holders are difficult to sell, or otherwise market.

Merger, Doctrine of – a doctrine that allows estates to merge, when successive vested estates are held by the same person. Merger can result in the holder of a life estate and vested remainder to hold a fee simple absolute. As one example, application of Shelley's Rule may trigger the Doctrine of Merger. See: Shelley's Rule.

Possibility of Reverter – a future interest created in the transferor upon the conveyance of a fee simple determinable. A possibility of reverter allows its holder to automatically repossess the estate upon the occurrence or nonoccurrence of the limiting event. A possibility of reverter can only be retained by the transferor (or the transferor's heirs), and cannot be created in a transferee. See: Fee Simple Determinable, Executory Interest.

Present Possessory Interest – an interest which is possessory, and which usually includes traditional property rights such as the right to possess, occupy, or exclude. The extent of the present possessory interest, in part, governs the extent of dominion and control. The shorter the possessory interest, the more weighty the rights of future interest holders. See: Waste, Doctrine of.

Remainder – a remainder is a future interest held by a grantee which (i) is capable of becoming possessory immediately upon the expiration of the prior estate and (ii) cannot divest any interest in a prior transferee. Remainders are freely alienable, inheritable, and devisable. A remainder cannot follow a vested fee simple. Remainders are either vested or contingent. See: Alternative Contingent Remainders; Contingent Remainder; Vested Remainder.

Reversion – the interest remaining in the transferor after conveying away less than his/her entire interest. A reversion will always follow a contingent remainder.

Right of Entry - a future interest created in the transferor upon the conveyance of a fee simple subject to condition subsequent. The right of entry represents the transferor's right to elect to repossess the estate upon the occurrence or nonoccurrence of the condition limiting the fee simple subject to condition subsequent. This right is subject to the doctrine of laches. In most jurisdictions, a right of entry is alienable, devisable, and inheritable, although some jurisdictions restrict the alienability of this interest.

Rule Against Perpetuities – a rule furthering marketability stating that no interest is valid if it has the potential to vest more than 21 years after the death of the lives in being at the creation of the interest. This rule is applied to contingent remainders, executory interests, and vested remainders subject to open. Classically, interests that violate this rule are blue-penciled (cancelled) out of the conveyance. Modernly, some form of wait-and-see approach is used in most jurisdictions. See: USRAP.

Rule of Construction – a rule of construction describes a doctrine that is applied only when it would facilitate the intention of the grantor. A rule of construction is not applied when it would frustrate the grantor's intent. See: Worthier Title, Doctrine of.

Rule of Law – a rule of law describes a doctrine that is applied regardless of the intention of the grantor. The doctrine is thus applied even when it would frustrate the grantor's intent.

Rules Furthering Marketability – rules which operate to further the alienablity of land. Conveyances can inhibit marketability by creating interests in unascertainable individuals who cannot market their interest. Rules Furthering Marketablity seek to transmute such interests and thereby enhance the market.

Shelley's Case – a doctrine that furthers marketability. If a freehold estate is transferred to a person, and, in the same instrument, a remainder is transferred to the heirs (or heirs of the body) of that person, that person takes both the freehold estate and the remainder. For this rule to apply, there must be (i) one instrument (ii) that creates a freehold estate in a transferee, and (iii) also creates a remainder in that transferee's heirs. The interests must both be legal or both equitable. Shelley's Case is a rule of law. See: Rules Furthering Marketability, Rule of Law.

Testamentary Transfer – a transfer made effective upon death, such as by will.

Term of Years – a leasehold interest created in a transferee for a duration specified in the grant. In some jurisdictions, a conveyance of an extremely long term of years is considered a grant of a fee simple. The doctrine of waste is applicable. Terms of years are alienable, devisable, and inheritable.

Trust, Transfers in - a conveyance of property in trust typically grants legal title to a trustee, who manages a property for the benefit of a beneficiary. The beneficiary often holds an equitable interest in the property.

Unascertainable Individual – an individual (or defined group) whose identity is not certain; often someone who is not in existence at the time of conveyance. Generally, one cannot point to an unascertainable individual. See: Ascertainable Individual.

USRAP – Uniform Statutory Rule Against Perpetuities. USRAP jurisdictions take a wait-and-see approach for a statutory period of 90 years.

Vested Remainder – a vested remainder is a remainder that is (i) not subject to any condition precedent (other than the natural termination of the preceding estate) <u>and</u> (ii) held by an ascertainable individual. See Remainder.

Waste – a doctrine which restricts the present possessor of an estate from using, spoiling, or exploiting the land in a way which would injure the interests of the future interest holders. This doctrine balances the present possessor's right to use against the future interest holder's right to receive. The less certain a future interest is to become possessory, the greater the allowable present use. The doctrine of waste does not apply to the holder of a defeasible fee.

Words of Condition – words of condition expressly state the condition which divests the transferee of a fee simple subject to condition subsequent. These words are traditionally: "provided that," "but if," and "on condition that."

Words of Duration – words of duration expressly state the condition which divests the transferee of a fee simple determinable. These words are traditionally: "as long as," "while," "until," and "during."

Words of Limitation – language in a conveyance which identifies the type of estate being created, thus setting the "limits" of the estate. See: Words of Purchase.

Words of Purchase – language in a conveyance which identifies the transferees of the interest, but which does not describe the type of estate transferred. See: Words of Limitation.

Worthier Title, Doctrine of – a rule furthering marketability. Where a conveyance creates a remainder (or an executory interest) in the transferor's own heirs, the transferor is deemed to have created a future interest in herself rather than in her heirs. In the United States, this rule does not apply to testamentary transfers. The Doctrine of Worthier Title is a rule of construction. See: Rule of Construction.

II. Present Possessory Estates

Fee Simple

The fee simple is the largest quantum estate that exists. It has the potential to endure forever. The owner of a fee simple has maximum control over the estate, with the ability to carve out of the fee simple a "lesser" estate and/or future interest. The present possessor of a fee simple has the right to use the estate without any limitation or condition. The estate is completely alienable, devisable, and inheritable.

The typical fee simple is created by a conveyance that reads "to X and his heirs". In most instances, the words "and his heirs" do not give the heirs any rights whatsoever; rather, they are words that are used solely to describe the extent of the estate. In technical terms, the words "and his heirs" function as words of limitation, rather than words of purchase. Thus, the conveyance "G –> Bart and his heirs" creates no interest in Bart's heirs. Rather the phrase "and his heirs" indicates that G has granted Bart a fee simple. When these words of limitation are present, the conveyance should be read as "G conveys to Bart in fee simple."

Before the 1600's, it was imperative to include the words "and his heirs" in the conveyance if the grantor wanted to convey a fee simple. If these words were not present, a life estate was presumed. However, at modern law, the words "and his heirs" are not necessary to create a fee simple. The presumption is that the grantor intends a fee simple unless the grantor uses words of limitation that expressly convey a different estate. This modern presumption reflects our social policy of enhancing and furthering an active market in real property by maximizing alienability. Thus, where the type of estate is ambiguous, a fee simple is presumed. Under modern presumptions, a conveyance that reads merely "to Bart" is sufficient to convey a fee simple.

Fee Simple Problems

1.   Kermit ➜ Ernie and his heirs.

T	

SoT	

2.   Ernie ➜ Bert.

T	

SoT	

1.   Kermit ➜ Ernie and his heirs.

T	Kermit to Ernie in <u>fee simple</u>
SoT	Ernie - fee simple

The words of purchase "to Ernie" denote Ernie as the grantee of the present possessory interest; thus, he receives the estate. The words of limitation "and his heirs" identify the estate as a fee simple.

Remember, Ernie's heirs have no interest. The words "and his heirs" are words of limitation, words that merely describe the estate. No interest in the estate is transferred to the heirs through these words.

Kermit no longer has an interest in the estate because a fee simple is the largest quantum estate. By granting Ernie a fee simple, Kermit retains nothing. Kermit has given away his entire interest.

2.   Ernie ➜ Bert.

T	Ernie to Bert in <u>fee simple</u>
SoT	Bert - fee simple

SoT (1600)	Bert - life estate
	Ernie - reversion

The words of purchase "to Bert" denote Bert as the grantee of the present possessory interest; thus, he receives the estate. There are no words of limitation, so a fee simple is presumed. Today, if the conveyance does not contain words which limit the estate, it is presumed the grantor conveyed the largest possible estate, a fee simple. This maximizes the property's alienability and allows its possessors the greatest flexibility.

In 1600, the words "and his heirs" were required to create a fee simple. At that time, a life estate was the preferred estate; thus, when the conveyance contained no such words, a life estate was deemed to be created.

3.   Ernie ➜ Bert in fee simple.

T	
SoT	

4.   Ernie ➜ Bert for life, and then to Kermit and his heirs.

T	
SoT	

3.   Ernie ➜ Bert in fee simple.

T	Ernie to Bert in <u>fee simple</u>	
SoT	Bert	- fee simple

SoT (1600)	Bert	- life estate
	Ernie	- reversion

The words of purchase "to Bert" denote Bert as the grantee of the present possessory interest; thus, he receives the estate. "In fee simple" are not words of limitation, but these words reflect Ernie's intent to give his entire interest to Bert. Today, the estate conveyed is a fee simple because of both the grantor's intention and the fact that a fee simple is the preferred estate.

In 1600, the words "and his heirs" were required to create a fee simple. At that time, a life estate was the preferred estate. Consequently, since the conveyance contained no such words, Bert would have received a life estate (and Ernie would have had a reversion because he has not conveyed away the entire estate), regardless of the grantor's intent.

4.   Ernie ➜ Bert for life, and then to Kermit and his heirs.

T	Ernie to Bert in <u>life estate</u>, then to Kermit in <u>fee simple</u>	
SoT	Bert	- life estate
	Kermit	- vested remainder in fee simple

The words of purchase "to Bert" denote Bert as the grantee of the present possessory interest; thus, he receives the estate. The words of limitation "for life" identify the estate as a life estate. Once the life estate ends, Kermit's interest becomes possessory.

The words of purchase "to Kermit" denote the grantee of the future interest. Kermit will receive the estate upon the expiration of the preceding estate. There are no words of limitation, so a fee simple is presumed. As you will learn, the interest is a remainder because (i) it is capable of becoming possessory immediately upon the expiration of the preceding estate and (ii) it cannot divest any other interests. It is a vested remainder because, at the time of the conveyance, Kermit is ascertainable (you can point to him) and there are no conditions precedent to his gaining possession.

5.   Ernie ➔ Bert for 100 years.

T	
SoT	

6.   Ernie ➔ Bert for ever and ever.

T	
SoT	

5.   Ernie ➜ Bert for 100 years.

T	Ernie to Bert for <u>a term of years</u>	
SoT	Bert Ernie	- term of years - reversion

The words of purchase "to Bert" denote Bert as the grantee of the present possessory interest; thus, he receives the estate. The words of limitation "for 100 years" identify the estate as a term of years. As you will learn, a term of years is an estate of fixed duration, in this instance lasting exactly 100 years. Many states now have limits on term of years so that they cannot exceed 99 years; if it does, the jurisdiction will sometimes read the conveyance as creating a fee simple in the grantee.

This is a not fee simple because a fee simple has an infinite duration whereas a term of years has a definite starting and stopping point. In this instance, the estate begins the day of conveyance and ends the last day of the one hundredth year. [However, in a jurisdiction where the maximum duration of a term of years is 99 years, the conveyance may be interpreted as conveying a fee simple.] Since Ernie did not convey his entire interest, he retains a reversion.

6.   Ernie ➜ Bert for ever and ever.

T	Ernie to Bert in <u>fee simple</u>	
SoT	Bert	- fee simple

SoT (1600)	Bert Ernie	- life estate - reversion

The words of purchase "to Bert" denote Bert as the grantee of the present possessory interest; thus, he receives the estate. The words "for ever and ever" are not words of limitation, but they reflect Ernie's intent to give his entire interest to Bert. Today, if the conveyance does not contain words that describe the estate, it is presumed the grantor conveyed the largest possible estate, a fee simple.

In 1600, the words "and his heirs" were required to create a fee simple. At that time, a life estate was the preferred estate. Thus, since the conveyance contained no such words, Bert would have received a life estate and Ernie would have retained a reversion, regardless of the grantor's intent.

7.   Ernie ➔ Luke, my pet dog, for ever and ever.

      Fact: Luke is a dog.

T	
SoT	

8.   Ernie ➔ Bert and his heirs upon Bert's marriage.

      Fact: Bert is not married.

T	
SoT	

7.   Ernie ➜ Luke, my pet dog, for ever and ever.

Fact: Luke is a dog.

T	No conveyance
SoT	Ernie retains a fee simple

Ernie retains a fee simple because the law does not recognize conveyances to animals, regardless of the intent of the grantor. Valid conveyees include, inter alia, human individuals, corporations, partnerships, and trustees of trusts.

8.   Ernie ➜ Bert and his heirs upon Bert's marriage.

Fact: Bert is not married.

T	Ernie to Bert in <u>fee simple</u> upon Bert's marriage	
SoT	Ernie	- fee simple on executory limitation
	Bert	- springing executory interest in fee simple

The words of purchase "to Bert" denote Bert as the grantee. The words of limitation "and his heirs" identify the estate as a fee simple; however, the condition of Bert's marriage must be fulfilled for Bert to gain possession of the estate.

When analyzing a conveyance, it is helpful to begin by determining who has present possession. Because Bert's interest only becomes possessory upon his marriage, Ernie has retained present possession. Bert's interest is a future interest [although future interests are present interests (they exist now), the label "future" interest indicates that possession is delayed until some future time).

As you will learn, Ernie retains a fee simple defeasible estate. (See Executory Interests). More specifically, Ernie has a fee simple on executory limitation. It is on executory limitation because possession will be transferred from Ernie to Bert when Bert gets married. Bert has a springing interest because Bert, the grantee, will divest Ernie, the grantor, of the estate.

9.   Ernie ➔ Bert for life.

T	
SoT	

10.   Ernie ➔ Bert and his heirs.

Fact: Bert has two children.

T	
SoT	

9.   Ernie ➔ Bert for life.

T	Ernie to Bert in <u>life estate</u>	
SoT	Bert Ernie	- life estate - reversion

The words of purchase "to Bert" denote Bert as the grantee of the present possessory interest; thus, he receives the estate. The words of limitation "for life" identify the estate as a life estate.

Since Ernie carved out a smaller estate (a life estate) from his larger estate (a fee simple), he retains a future interest known as a reversion, which will become possessory upon the expiration of the life estate.

10.   Ernie ➔ Bert and his heirs.

        Fact: Bert has two children.

T	Ernie to Bert in <u>fee simple</u>
SoT	Bert - fee simple

The words of purchase "to Bert" denote Bert as the grantee of the present possessory interest; thus, he receives the estate. The words of limitation "and his heirs" identify the estate as a fee simple.

The conveyance reads, "Ernie to Bert in fee simple." Bert's children receive nothing by the conveyance; they have no interest even though they are Bert's heirs apparent (Bert has no heirs until he dies). The only way Bert's children can gain an interest in the estate is for Bert to convey or devise the estate to them, or through intestate succession.

Life Estate

Creation of the Estate

A life estate is an estate whose duration is measured by a particular human life. Upon the death of the measuring life, the estate terminates. The traditional words of limitation used to create a life estate are the words "for life". Other words may be used to the same effect, so long as they demonstrate the intent to create a life estate [such as "until … dies" or "while ... is alive"]. If the grantor transfers "to Homer for life," Homer has a present possessory interest in an estate for life. Upon Homer's death, the estate terminates.

When the duration of a life estate is measured by the life of a person other than the grantee, the estate is referred to as an estate per autre vie (for the life of another). If the grantor transfers "to Homer for the life of Marge," Homer has a present possessory interest in an estate for life, measured by Marge's life. Homer has a life estate per autre vie. Upon Marge's death, Homer's estate will terminate.

Life estates may be created so that they end prematurely upon the happening of a certain event. This is known as a defeasible life estate. Greg can grant Greenacre "to Ann for life as long as Ann uses it as a farm." Because Ann's life estate may be cut short by Ann's failure to meet the usage restriction, Ann is said to have a defeasible life estate. Translated, this conveyance reads "Greg to Ann in life estate defeasible" (as long as Ann uses it as a farm)". At the time of this conveyance, Greg retains a reversion. Greg's reversion will become possessory at the earlier of (i) Ann's failing to use the property as a farm or (ii) at the time of Ann's death.

Alienability

A life estate is alienable. Since a life estate terminates upon the death of the grantee, it is neither devisable nor inheritable.

If a life estate is alienated, the grantee of the life estate receives a "life estate per autre vie." The new owner of the life estate gets an estate measured by the original grantee's life. For example, "Greg to Ann for life" creates a life estate in Ann, with a reversion in Greg. If Ann conveys her life estate to Bill with the words, "I give all my interest to Bill," Ann has given Bill a life estate per autre vie. Bill has the possessory interest for as long as Ann lives; when Ann dies, Greg's reversion becomes possessory. Greg's interest is not changed by Ann's grant to Bill. Regardless of how long Bill lives, the life estate Bill possesses will end when Ann dies. If Bill predeceases Ann, his life estate per autre vie will pass by his will or through intestate succession to his successors [Therefore, if Bill (the holder of a life estate per autre vie) dies, but Ann is still alive, the life estate per autre vie continues and will be held either by Bill's devisees (his testate successors) or by Bill's heirs (his intestate successors).]

Life Estates and Future Interests

If the holder of a fee simple conveys a life estate, a future interest will always follow. Future interests that can follow a life estate are reversions, remainders, and executory interests. A reversion is a future interest in the grantor which can become possessory upon the expiration of the life estate. A remainder is a future interest in a third party which also can become possessory upon the expiration of the life estate. An executory interest is a future interest in a third party which normally cuts short the life estate.

Note that while the interest that follows the life estate is called a future interest, the grantee holds the interest now. Therefore, it is a present interest; only possession is delayed until the future.

Waste

The holder of a life estate is subject to the doctrine of waste. This doctrine imposes restrictions upon the life estate holder's right of use; it creates a duty to use the land in such a way as not to injure unduly the rights of the future interest holders whose interests will become possessory upon the expiration of the life estate. The key focus of the doctrine of waste is to protect those who hold future interests from unreasonable interference with their interest by the life estate holder. If Greg conveys Forestacre "to Ann for life, then to Bill and his heirs," Ann gains present possession (a life estate) and Bill has a future interest (a remainder in fee simple). If Forestacre is a property forested with trees, the doctrine of waste prevents Ann from cutting down trees at her personal whim. Ann's free use of the land is restrained by Bill's interest in succeeding to a possessory estate that still has value. Ann may not waste the property by cutting down all the trees and gaining the complete economic advantage of the land. (But note, there was at common law an exception for the cutting of trees in order to clear land for cultivation.) Bill's interest, although not possessory until the future, still restrains the present user from unduly interfering with the parcel's inherent value. If Ann's actions while she is in possession of her life estate unreasonably interfere with the value of Bill's remainder, Bill has an action in waste against Ann.

Life Estate Problems

1.   Homer ➔ Marge for life.

T	
SoT	

2.   Homer ➔ Marge for as long as Marge lives.

T	
SoT	

1.   Homer ➔ Marge for life.

T	Homer to Marge in <u>life estate</u>
SoT	Marge - life estate Homer - reversion

The words of purchase "to Marge" denote Marge as the grantee of the present possessory interest; thus, she receives the estate. The words of limitation "for life" identify the estate as a life estate.

Since Homer carved out a smaller estate from his larger fee simple, he retains a future interest known as a reversion, which will become possessory upon the expiration of the life estate.

2.   Homer ➔ Marge for as long as Marge lives.

T	Homer to Marge in <u>life estate</u>
SoT	Marge - life estate Homer - reversion

The words of purchase "to Marge" denote Marge as the grantee of the present possessory interest; thus, she receives the estate. There are no traditional words of limitation present in the conveyance; however, the words "for as long as Marge lives" identify the grantor's intent to create a life estate. Thus, Marge receives a life estate.

Since Homer carved out a smaller estate from his larger fee simple, he retains a future interest known as a reversion, which will become possessory upon the expiration of the life estate.

3.　　Homer ➔ Marge until she dies.

T	
SoT	

4.　　Homer ➔ Apple Computer, Inc. for life.

T	
SoT	

3.   Homer ➔ Marge until she dies.

T	Homer to Marge in <u>life estate</u>	
SoT	Marge Homer	- life estate - reversion

The words of purchase "to Marge" denote Marge as the grantee of the present possessory interest; thus, she receives the estate. There are no traditional words of limitation present in the conveyance; however, the words "until she dies" identify the grantor's intent to create a life estate. Thus, Marge receives a life estate.

Since Homer carved out a smaller estate from his larger fee simple, he retains a future interest known as a reversion, which will become possessory upon the expiration of the life estate.

4.   Homer ➔ Apple Computer, Inc. for life.

T	No conveyance
SoT	Homer retains his fee simple

Homer retains his fee simple. Life estates cannot be created in favor of partnerships or corporations because they have a potentially infinite "lifetime."

5.   Homer ➔ Marge for life, then to Bart and his heirs.

T	
SoT	

6.   Homer ➔ Marge for her use during her lifetime, then to Marge's heirs.

T	
SoT	

5.　　　Homer ➔ Marge for life, then to Bart and his heirs.

T	Homer to Marge in <u>life estate</u>, then to Bart in <u>fee simple</u>
SoT	Marge　　　　- life estate Bart　　　　　- vested remainder in fee simple

The words of purchase "to Marge" denote Marge as the grantee of the present possessory interest; thus, she receives the estate. The words of limitation "for life" identify the estate as a life estate.

The words of purchase "to Bart" denote Bart as the grantee of a future interest. The words of limitation "and his heirs" identify the estate (that will exist when the future interest becomes possessory) as a fee simple. The interest is a remainder because (i) it is capable of becoming possessory immediately upon the expiration of the preceding estate and (ii) it cannot divest any other interests. It is vested because Bart is ascertainable at the time of the conveyance and there is no condition precedent. (See Remainders.)

Homer retains no interest because he has given away everything he owns.

6.　　　Homer ➔ Marge for her use during her lifetime, then to Marge's heirs.

T	Homer to Marge in <u>life estate</u>, then to Marge's heirs in <u>fee simple</u>
SoT	Marge　　　　　　- life estate Marge's heirs　　- contingent remainder in fee simple Homer　　　　　- reversion

The words of purchase "to Marge" denote Marge as the grantee of the present possessory interest; thus, she receives the estate. There are no traditional words of limitation present in the conveyance; however, the words "for her use during her lifetime" identify the grantor's intent to create a life estate. Thus, Marge receives a life estate.

The words of purchase "to Marge's heirs" denote the grantee(s) of a future interest. There are no words of limitation, so a fee simple is presumed. The interest is a remainder because (i) it is capable of becoming possessory immediately upon the expiration of the preceding estate and (ii) it cannot divest any other interests. It is a contingent remainder because, at the time of the conveyance, Marge's heirs are unascertainable (an individual's heirs are only ascertained once the individual dies).

Homer retains a future interest known as a reversion. A reversion always follows a contingent remainder because someone must hold seisin in the estate at all times. Since a contingent remainder is not certain to vest, the grantor must retain a reversion.

7. Homer ➔ Marge for 99 years.

T	
SoT	

8. Homer ➔ Marge for Homer's life, then to Lisa for life, then to Bart and his heirs.

T	
SoT	

8(a) Marge dies during Homer's lifetime.

7.   Homer ➜ Marge for 99 years.

T	Homer to Marge for <u>a term of years</u>	
SoT	Marge Homer	- term of years - reversion

The words of purchase "to Marge" denote Marge as the grantee of the present possessory interest; thus, she receives the estate. The words of limitation "for 99 years" identify the estate as a term of years. The estate is a term of years because it has a definite calendar beginning and ending point, whereas a life estate is measured by a human life. Thus, Marge (or her grantees, devisees, or heirs) will continue to hold present possessory interest in the land for 99 years, regardless of when Marge dies.

Since Homer carved out a smaller estate (a term of years) from his larger estate (a fee simple), he retains a future interest known as a reversion, which will become possessory upon the expiration of the term of years. Homer (or his grantees, devisees, or heirs) will gain possession of the estate at the end of 99 years. If Marge dies before the end of the term, her grantees, devisees, or heirs will gain possession of the estate for the remaining period of the term.

8.   Homer ➜ Marge for Homer's life, then to Lisa for life, then to Bart and his heirs.

T	Homer to Marge in <u>life estate per autre vie</u>, then to Lisa in <u>life estate</u>, then to Bart in <u>fee simple</u>	
SoT	Marge Lisa Bart	- life estate per autre vie - vested remainder in life estate - vested remainder in fee simple

The words of purchase "to Marge" denote Marge as the grantee of the present possessory interest; thus, she receives the estate. The words of limitation "for Homer's life" identify Marge's estate as a life estate per autre vie (per another's life). Marge has a life estate measured by the length of Homer's life. When Homer dies, Marge's interest ceases.

The words of purchase "to Lisa" denote Lisa as the grantee of a future interest. The words of limitation "for life" identify Lisa's estate (that will exist if the future interest becomes possessory) as a life estate, based on her own life. The interest is a remainder because (i) it is capable of becoming possessory immediately upon the expiration of the preceding estate and (ii) it cannot divest any other interests. It is vested because Lisa is ascertainable at the time of the conveyance and there is no condition precedent.

The words of purchase "to Bart" denote Bart as the grantee of a future interest. The words of limitation "and his heirs" identify the estate (that will exist when the future interest becomes possessory) as a fee simple. The interest is a remainder because (i) it is capable of becoming possessory immediately upon the expiration of the preceding estate and (ii) it cannot divest any other interests. It is vested because Bart is ascertainable at the time of the conveyance and there is no condition precedent.

8(a)   Marge dies during Homer's lifetime.

Marge's interest endures as long as Homer is alive because Marge's interest is based on Homer's life, not her own. Since Homer is still alive at Marge's death, the estate would pass through Marge's will to her devisees or by intestacy to Marge's heirs. Lisa and Bart's interests are not affected. Lisa will gain possession upon Homer's death.

9.   Homer ➔ Marge for life, then to Bart.

T	
SoT	

9 (a)   Marge ➔ Lisa all my interest in Greenacre.

Facts: In a previous conveyance, Marge received a life estate in Greenacre from Homer. In the same conveyance, Homer gave his remainder to Bart.

T	
SoT	

i.   Marge dies.

ii.   Lisa dies during Marge's lifetime.

9.   Homer ➔ Marge for life, then to Bart.

T	Homer to Marge in <u>life estate</u>, then to Bart in <u>fee simple</u>	
SoT	Marge Bart	- life estate - vested remainder in fee simple

The words of purchase "to Marge" denote Marge as the grantee of the present possessory interest; thus, she receives the estate. The words of limitation "for life" identify the estate as a life estate.

The words of purchase "to Bart" denote Bart as the grantee of a future interest. There are no words of limitation, so a fee simple is presumed. The interest is a remainder because (i) it is capable of becoming possessory immediately upon the expiration of the preceding estate and (ii) it cannot divest any other interests. It is vested because Bart is ascertainable at the time of the conveyance and there is no condition precedent.

Homer has retained nothing of his previous fee simple because he conveyed away all that he owned.

9(a)   Marge ➔ Lisa all my interest in Greenacre.

Facts: In the previous conveyance, Marge received a life estate in Greenacre from Homer. In the same conveyance, Homer gave a remainder to Bart.

T	Marge to Lisa in <u>life estate per autre vie</u>	
SoT	Lisa Marge	- life estate per autre vie - has no interest

The words of purchase "to Lisa" denote Lisa as the grantee of the present possessory interest; thus, she receives the estate. When the grantor has a life estate and she conveys all she has, the grantee receives a life estate measured by the grantor's life. Therefore, Lisa has a life estate per autre vie (per another's life).

i.   Marge dies.

Lisa's interest endures only so long as Marge is alive. When Marge dies, Lisa's life estate per autre vie ends. Bart's remainder then becomes possessory.

ii.   Lisa dies during Marge's lifetime.

Lisa's interest is based on Marge's life, not her own; therefore, upon Lisa's death, the estate would pass through Lisa's will to her devisees or by intestacy to Lisa's heirs. Marge has no interest because she conveyed away everything she owned to Lisa. Bart's interest is not affected because his interest does not become possessory until Marge's death.

10.   Homer ➔ Marge for Lisa's life.

T	
SoT	

10(a). Marge sells her interest to Zack. One year later, Zack dies and wills all of his assets to Mellonie.

T	
SoT	

10.   Homer ➔ Marge for Lisa's life.

T	Homer to Marge in <u>life estate per autre vie</u>	
SoT	Marge Homer	- life estate per autre vie - reversion

The words of purchase "to Marge" denote Marge as the grantee of the present possessory interest; thus, she receives the estate. The words of limitation "for Lisa's life" identify Marge's interest as a life estate per autre vie (per another's life). Marge has a life estate measured by the length of Lisa's life. When Lisa dies, Marge's interest ceases.

Since Homer carved out a smaller estate from his larger fee simple, he retains a future interest known as a reversion, which will become possessory upon the expiration of the life estate.

10(a). Marge sells her interest to Zack. One year later, Zack dies and wills all of his assets to Mellonie.

T	Marge to Zack in <u>life estate per autre vie</u>.	
SoT	Zack Homer	- life estate per autre vie - reversion

Upon Zack's death...

SoT	Mellonie Homer	- life estate per autre vie - reversion

The words of purchase "to Zack" denote Zack as the grantee of the present possessory interest; thus, he receives the estate. When the grantor has a life estate and she conveys all that she has, the grantee receives a life estate measured by the grantor's life. In this case, the interest that Marge holds is a life estate per autre vie measured by the life of Lisa. This is the interest that is sold to Zack. In most jurisdictions, the life estate per autre vie is freely alienable, devisable, and inheritable. Therefore, Zack receives a possessory interest measured by Lisa's life. When Zack dies, the life estate per autre vie goes to Mellonie pursuant to Zack's will.

Since Homer carved out a smaller estate from his larger fee simple, he retains a future interest known as a reversion, which will become possessory upon the expiration of the life estate (measured by Lisa's life).

Fee Tail

Creation of the Estate

A fee tail provides present possession to the grantee and his direct lineal descendants, so long as the grantee's bloodline continues. At common law, a fee tail was created by the words "to Albert and the heirs of his body." The words "to Albert" are words of purchase, describing to whom the estate is conveyed. The words "and the heirs of his body" are words of limitation, words that identify the estate as a fee tail.

Ex: Fred ➜ Betty and the heirs of her body.

T	Fred to Betty in <u>fee tail</u>	
SoT	Betty Fred	- fee tail - reversion

The words of purchase "to Betty" denote Betty as the grantee of the present possessory interest; thus, she receives the present estate. The words of limitation "and the heirs of her body" identify the estate as a fee tail. Fred retains a reversion (a future interest in the grantor) that will become possessory if, and when, Betty's line of lineal descendants should ever expire.

Nature of the Estate

If Betty has a fee tail, Betty has a present possessory interest in the estate for the duration of her life (Betty has present possession of the estate; Betty also has the right to future possession until her death). Upon Betty's death, the estate is inherited by Betty's lineal descendants (her children, then grandchildren, then great grandchildren ...). If and when Betty's lineal descendants expire, the estate will revert to the grantor or the grantor's devisees or heirs.

When Fred, the holder of the fee simple, conveys a fee tail, he does not convey away his whole interest in the estate. Fred retains a reversion, which is a future interest. Fred's reversion may become possessory if Betty's direct bloodline ever ends. Since the fee tail estate can only pass to the lineal heirs of Betty, there may be a time when Betty's direct line of descendants "dries up" (i.e., Betty has no children, or her children have no children, or... her grandchildren have no children ...). The estate will then revert back to Fred, the grantor. If Fred is not alive, it will go to Fred's estate and pass pursuant to Fred's will or through intestate succession.

Alienability

A fee tail has limited alienability. Betty may alienate only her right to possession until her death. When death occurs, regardless of who is in possession, the estate passes to Betty's lineal heirs. [At common law, under the strictures of primogenitor, the estate went to the eldest son.]

A fee tail is not devisable. Betty does not have the right to leave her estate by will. On her death, the property interest automatically passes to her direct lineal heir.

A fee tail is inheritable - in a modified way. It is restricted to the lineal descendants of Betty, the grantee. Upon Betty's death, only her lineal heirs are entitled to inherit the estate.

Manipulating the Tail

Successors to the fee tail can be restricted to a particular group of lineal descendants of the grantee.

Ex: Fred ➜ Sue and the male heirs of her body.

T	Fred to Sue in <u>fee tail male</u>
SoT	Sue - fee tail male Fred - reversion

The words of purchase "to Sue" denote Sue as the grantee of the present possessory interest; thus, she receives the estate. The words of limitation "and the male heirs of her body" describe the estate as a fee tail male. When Sue dies, her estate can only pass to her male lineal heirs. Therefore, if Sue has two sons and one daughter, upon Sue's death, the sons gain the present possessory interest in fee tail while the daughter gains no interest. The estate will then pass only to the males in the sons' lines of descent.

Ex: Fred ➜ Herman and the female heirs of his body.

T	Fred to Herman in <u>fee tail female</u>
SoT	Herman - fee tail female Fred - reversion

The words of purchase "to Herman" denote Herman as the grantee of the present possessory interest; thus, he receives the estate. The words of limitation "and the female heirs of his body" identify the estate as a fee tail female. Upon Herman's death, the estate will pass only to the females in his line of descendants, and to their female descendants upon their deaths.

Ex: Fred ➜ Wilma and the heirs of her body by Fred.

T	Fred to Wilma in <u>fee tail special</u>
SoT	Wilma - fee tail special Fred - reversion

The words of purchase "to Wilma" denote Wilma as the grantee of the present possessory interest; thus, she receives the estate. The words of limitation "and the heirs of her body by Fred" identify the estate as a fee tail special. A fee tail special is created when the grantor wants to restrict the possessory interest not only to the lineal heirs of the grantee, but also to those lineal heirs parented by a second individual (here Fred). The typical goal of this type of conveyance is to keep the property within the immediate family bloodline.

Modern Day Fee Tail

Today, most states have legislation that has the practical effect of precluding, or limiting, the creation of a fee tail. There are four major jurisdictional approaches:

1. Many jurisdictions convert what would have been a fee tail under common law into a fee simple in the first grantee. Thus, a grant to "Bob and the heirs of his body" creates a fee simple in Bob.

2. Some jurisdictions convert the fee tail into a life estate in the first grantee, with a remainder in fee simple to the lineal descendants of the first taker.

3. Some jurisdictions provide that the first taker acquires a fee tail, but that the lineal descendants of the first taker acquire a fee simple.

4. A few states (Delaware, Maine, Massachusetts, and Rhode Island) still allow the creation of fee tails. These states recognize a fee tail as it existed at common law; however, the holder of the fee tail has the power to transmute the fee tail into a fee simple by conveying away his/her interest by deed. This process is called disentailing. Note, in these jurisdictions, the holder of the fee tail cannot transfer the estate by will.

Fee Tail Problems

1.   Barney ➔ Fred and the heirs of his body.

T	
SoT	

2.   Barney ➔ Fred and the heirs of his body by Wilma.

T	
SoT	

1.   Barney ➜ Fred and the heirs of his body.

T	Barney to Fred in <u>fee tail</u>
SoT	Fred - fee tail Barney - reversion

The words of purchase "to Fred" denote Fred as the grantee of the present possessory interest; thus, he receives the estate. The words of limitation "and the heirs of his body" identify the estate as a fee tail in those jurisdictions recognizing the estate.

Since Barney carved out a smaller estate from his larger fee simple, he retains a future interest known as reversion. Barney's interest will become possessory if the issue line of Fred ceases.

2.   Barney ➜ Fred and the heirs of his body by Wilma.

T	Barney to Fred in <u>fee tail special</u>
SoT	Fred - fee tail special Barney - reversion

The words of purchase "to Fred" denote Fred as the grantee of the present possessory interest; thus, he receives the estate. The words of limitation "and the heirs of his body" identify the estate as a fee tail in those jurisdictions recognizing the estate. The words "by Wilma" place a particular condition on who may gain a possessory interest in the estate (here, issue that share Wilma's genes, as well as Fred's), creating a fee tail special.

Since Barney carved out a smaller estate from his larger fee simple, he retains a future interest known as reversion. Barney's interest will become possessory if the issue line of Fred and Wilma ceases.

3.   Barney ➜ Fred and his children.

T	
SoT	

4.   Barney ➜ Fred for life, then to his first child Pebbles for life, then to Pebbles' first born child for life.

       Fact: Pebbles has no children.

T	
SoT	

3.   Barney ➜ Fred and his children.

T	Barney to Fred and his children in <u>fee simple</u>
SoT	Fred and his children - fee simple

The words of purchase "to Fred and his children" denote Fred and his children as the grantees of the present possessory interest; thus, they receive the estate. There are no words of limitation, so a fee simple is presumed.

The words "and his children" are not words of limitation; therefore, no fee tail is created (generally, the grantor must use the words "heirs of body"). Again, the fact that terms may have the same or similar colloquial meanings has little bearing on the formalities governing estates. To create a fee tail, the conveyance must contain precise terms ("and the heirs of his/her body") specifying unequivocally that a fee tail is intended.

4.   Barney ➜ Fred for life, then to his first child Pebbles for life, then to Pebbles' first born
          child for life.

          Fact: Pebbles has no children.

T	Barney to Fred in <u>life estate</u>, then to Pebbles in <u>life estate</u>, then to Pebbles' first born child in <u>life estate</u>
SoT	Fred - life estate Pebbles - vested remainder in life estate Pebbles' first born - contingent remainder in life estate Barney - reversion

The words of purchase "to Fred" denote Fred as the grantee of the present possessory interest; thus, he receives the estate. The words of limitation "for life" identify the estate as a life estate.

The words of purchase "to Pebbles" denote Pebbles as the grantee of a future interest. The words of limitation "for life" identify the interest as a life estate. Pebbles' future interest is a remainder because (i) it is capable of becoming possessory immediately upon the expiration of the preceding estate and (ii) it cannot divest any other interests. It is vested because Pebbles is ascertainable at the time of the conveyance and there is no condition precedent to her receiving the estate.

The words of purchase "to Pebbles' first born child" denote Pebbles' first born as the grantee of a future interest. The words of limitation "for life" identify the estate as a life estate. Pebbles' first born's future interest is a remainder because (i) it is capable of becoming possessory immediately upon the expiration of the preceding estate and (ii) it cannot divest any other interests. It is a contingent remainder because, at the time of the conveyance, the first born child of Pebbles is unascertainable (the child is not yet born).

Although his conveyance describes the general effect of a fee tail, no fee tail is created because it does not contain the words "and the heirs of his/her body". Instead, Barney has created three successive life estates. Since Barney has not given away his entire interest, he retains a reversion. The reversion will become possessory at the end of Pebbles' first born child's life estate, or, in the event that Pebbles remains childless, Barney (or his devisees or heirs) will receive the estate upon the expiration of Pebbles' life estate.

5.   Barney ➔ Fred and the heirs of his body named Pebbles.

T	
SoT	

6.   Mr. Slate ➔ Fred for life, then to Fred's nephews and the heirs of their bodies that are female.

Fact: Fred has no nephews

T	
SoT	

5.   Barney ➔ Fred and the heirs of his body named Pebbles.

T	Barney to Fred in <u>fee tail Pebbles</u>	
SoT	Fred Barney	- fee tail Pebbles - reversion

The words of purchase "to Fred" denote Fred as the grantee of the present possessory interest; thus, he receives the estate. The words of limitation "and the heirs of his body" identify the estate as a fee tail in those jurisdictions recognizing the estate. The words "named Pebbles" place a particular condition on which descendants may gain a possessory interest in the estate, creating a fee tail Pebbles.

Since Barney carved out a smaller estate from his larger fee simple, he retains a future interest known as a reversion. Barney's interest will become possessory if, and when, Fred produces no descendants named Pebbles.

6.   Mr. Slate ➔ Fred for life, then to Fred's nephews and the heirs of their bodies that are female.

       Fact: Fred has no nephews.

T	Mr. Slate to Fred in <u>life estate</u>, then to Fred's nephews in <u>fee tail female</u>	
SoT	Fred Fred's nephews Mr. Slate	- life estate - contingent remainder in fee tail female - reversion

The words of purchase "to Fred" denote Fred as the grantee of the present possessory interest; thus, he receives the estate. The words of limitation "for life" identify the estate as a life estate.

The words of purchase "to Fred's nephews" denote them as the grantees of a future interest. The words of limitation "and the heirs of their bodies" identify the estate as a fee tail in jurisdictions recognizing the estate. The words "that are female" place a particular condition on which descendants can gain a possessory interest in the estate, creating a fee tail female. It is a remainder because (i) it is capable of becoming possessory immediately upon the expiration of the preceding estate and (ii) it cannot divest any other interests. It is contingent because, at the time of the conveyance, Fred's nephews are unascertainable (they are not yet born).

Since Mr. Slate carved out a smaller estate from his larger fee simple, he retains a future interest known as a reversion. Mr. Slate's interest will become possessory if, and when, Fred dies without ever having had a nephew, or at the expiration of Fred's nephews' female lineal descendants.

7.   Barney ➔ Betty and the female heirs of her body by Barney.

T	
SoT	

8.   Barney ➔ Betty for life, then to Wilma and the children of her body.

Fact: Wilma has one child.

T	
SoT	

7.   Barney ➔ Betty and the female heirs of her body by Barney.

T	Barney to Betty in <u>fee tail special female</u>
SoT	Betty - fee tail special female Barney - reversion

The words of purchase "to Betty" denote Betty as the grantee of the present possessory interest; thus, she receives the estate. The words of limitation "and the female heirs of her body" identify the estate as a fee tail in those jurisdictions recognizing the estate. The words "by Barney" place a condition on who may gain a possessory interest in the estate (they must share Barney's genes), creating a fee tail special. An added condition is that Betty's heirs by Barney must be female.

Since Barney carved out a smaller estate from his larger fee simple, he retains a future interest known as a reversion. Barney's interest will become possessory if there are no female heirs of Betty and Barney.

8.   Barney ➔ Betty for life, then to Wilma and the children of her body.

    Fact: Wilma has one child.

T	Barney to Betty in <u>life estate</u>, then to Wilma and her children in <u>fee simple</u>
SoT	Betty - life estate Wilma and… - vested remainder in fee simple subject to open

The words of purchase "to Betty" denote Betty as the grantee of the present possessory interest; thus, she receives the estate. The words of limitation "for life" identify the estate as a life estate.

The words of purchase "to Wilma and the children of her body" denote Wilma and her natural children as the grantees of a future interest. There are no words of limitation, so a fee simple is presumed. [Note, "and the children of her body" are not words creating a fee tail; generally, the grantor must use the words "heirs of body".] The interest is a remainder because (i) it is capable of becoming possessory immediately upon the expiration of the preceding estate and (ii) it cannot divest any other interests. It is vested because one Wilma and her child are ascertainable and there is no condition precedent. It is subject to open because Wilma can have more children.

9.   Barney ➔ Wilma for three years, then to Bam Bam and the heirs of his body.

T	
SoT	

10.   Barney ➔ Betty for life, then to Pebbles and the heirs of her body if Pebbles gets married.

T	
SoT	

9.   Barney ➔ Wilma for three years, then to Bam Bam and the heirs of his body.

T	Barney to Wilma for <u>a term of years</u>, then to Bam Bam in <u>fee tail</u>
SoT	Wilma - term of years Bam Bam - vested remainder in fee tail Barney - reversion

The words of purchase "to Wilma" denote Wilma as the grantee of the present possessory interest; thus, she receives the estate. The words of limitation "for three years" identify the estate as a term of years.

The words of purchase "to Bam Bam" denote Bam Bam as the grantee of a future interest. The words of limitation "and the heirs of his body" identify the estate (that will exist when the future interest becomes possessory) as a fee tail. Bam Bam has a remainder because (i) it is capable of becoming possessory immediately upon the expiration of the preceding estate and (ii) it cannot divest any other interests. It is vested because (i) Bam Bam is ascertainable [you can point to him] and (ii) there is no condition precedent to Bam Bam's gaining possession.

Since Barney carved out a smaller estate (a term of years + fee tail) from his larger estate (a fee simple), he retains a future interest know as a reversion. Barney's interest will become possessory if, and when, Wilma's term of years is completed and Bam Bam's direct line of descendants dies out.

10.   Barney ➔ Betty for life, then to Pebbles and the heirs of her body if Pebbles gets married.

T	Barney to Betty in <u>life estate</u>, then to Pebbles in <u>fee tail</u> if she marries
SoT	Betty - life estate Pebbles - contingent remainder in fee tail Barney - reversion

The words of purchase "to Betty" denote Betty as the grantee of the present possessory interest; thus, she receives the estate. The words of limitation "for life" identify the estate as a life estate.

The words of purchase "to Pebbles" denote Pebbles as the grantee of a future interest. The words of limitation "and the heirs of her body" identify the estate as a fee tail in those jurisdictions recognizing the estate. Pebbles has a remainder because (i) it is capable of becoming possessory immediately upon the expiration of the preceding estate and (ii) it cannot divest any other interests. It is a contingent remainder because it is subject to the condition precedent that Pebbles gets married.

Since Barney carved out a smaller estate (a life estate + fee tail) from his larger estate (a fee simple), he retains a future interest known as a reversion. Following Betty's term of years, Barney's interest will become possessory (i) if Pebbles does not marry or (ii) if, and when, Pebbles' direct line of descendants dies out.

Fee Simple Defeasible

A defeasible fee simple is a fee simple estate that may continue forever or may come to an end upon the occurrence of a stated future event. The defeasible fee simple encompasses a family of fee simple interests: the fee simple determinable, the fee simple subject to condition subsequent, and the fee simple on executory limitation. This problem set will review two types of fee simple defeasibles: the fee simple determinable and the fee simple subject to condition subsequent.

> A third type of defeasible fee is the fee simple on executory limitation. This estate can be distinguished from the fee simple determinable and the fee simple subject to condition subsequent because a fee simple on executory limitation is subject to divestment in favor of a person other than the grantor. When a defeasible fee is followed by an interest in a third party, the fee holder has a fee simple on executory limitation and the third party has an executory interest (e.g., Sam to "Diane as long as it is used as a school, then to Frazier.") This type of defeasible fee is discussed in the problem set on executory interests.

Fee Simple Determinable (FSD)

A fee simple determinable is a fee simple estate created in a grantee that <u>automatically</u> reverts to the grantor when a certain event or condition either occurs or fails to occur. In effect, the grantor has conveyed a fee simple in which the duration of the estate will be limited if a specified event happens.

The language of the conveyance must contain words of duration, which introduce the condition or event that will divest the grantee of the estate. The following words of duration are traditionally used to create a fee simple determinable: "as long as," "while," "until," and "during." Language in the conveyance that merely expresses the grantor's motive for conveying the estate will not create a fee simple determinable.

Ex: Sam ➔ Diane and her heirs as long as it is used as a school.

T	Sam to Diane in <u>fee simple</u> **as long as** (determinable) it is used as a school	
SoT	Diane Sam	- fee simple determinable - possibility of reverter

The words of purchase "to Diane" denote Diane as the grantee; thus, she receives the estate. The words of limitation "and her heirs" identify the estate as a fee simple. The words of duration "as long as" are words which create a fee simple determinable, a type of defeasible fee. The estate can be cut short upon the occurrence of the specified condition; Diane's fee simple will be cut short if the property ceases to be used as a school.

A possibility of reverter is always retained by the grantor when the grantor conveys a fee simple determinable estate. A possibility of reverter is a future interest retained by the grantor that automatically becomes possessory upon the happening of the stated condition. In the above example, when the property ceases to be used as a school, Diane's fee automatically ends and Sam (or his heirs or devisees) immediately becomes the present possessory fee owner. Sam's present possession is established by operation of law immediately upon the cessation of the property's use as a school. Sam does not have to do anything. The possessory interest automatically becomes his.

A possibility of reverter can only be retained by the grantor (or the grantor's heirs) and cannot be created in a grantee. Originally, under the common law, a possibility of reverter could not be devised or assigned; it could only be inherited. Today, in most jurisdictions, a possibility of reverter is freely alienable, devisable, and inheritable.

Fee Simple Subject to Condition Subsequent

A fee simple subject to condition subsequent is an estate created in a grantee that may be terminated at the grantor's election when a certain condition or event either occurs or fails to occur. If the condition is broken, the grantor has the power to terminate the estate by asserting the grantor's right of entry.

The language of the conveyance must contain words of condition which expressly state a condition or event that can work to divest the grantee of the estate. The words of condition should be actual words that signal divestment of the grantee, rather than merely state a motive for the grantor's conveyance of the estate. The following words of condition are traditionally used to create a fee simple subject to condition subsequent: "provided that," "but if," and "on condition that." To avoid ambiguity, the conveyance should also contain a clause that states "the grantor has a right to re-enter and reclaim".

Ex: Sam ➔ Diane and her heirs provided that, if the property is not used as a school, Sam shall have a right to re-enter and reclaim the land.

	Sam to Diane in <u>fee simple</u> **provided that** (subject to condition subsequent) if the property is not used as a school, Sam shall have the right to reenter and reclaim]
T	
SoT	Diane - fee simple subject to condition subsequent Sam - right of entry

The words of purchase "to Diane" denote Diane as grantee; thus, she receives the estate. The words of limitation "and her heirs" identify the estate as a fee simple. The words of condition "provided that" are words of limitation that create a fee simple subject to condition subsequent, a type of defeasible fee. The grantor may divest the grantee if the specified event happens. Thus, if the property is not used for a school, Sam can enter and assert his right to possession of the estate. Before, and until, Sam reenters, Diane continues as fee simple owner.

The grantor always retains a right of entry (also known as a right of re-entry or a power of termination) when the grantor conveys a fee simple subject to a condition subsequent. When the condition expressed in the conveyance occurs, the grantor may elect to "re-enter" the property and divest the grantee of possession. However, unlike a possibility of reverter, a right of entry does not automatically deprive the grantee of the estate. Until the grantor properly exercises the grantor's right of entry, the grantee's fee simple estate continues, despite the breach of the condition. The grantor is not compelled to divest the grantee.

In some states, the doctrine of laches will limit the amount of time the grantor has to enforce her right to possession once the condition is breached. Laches will bar the enforcement of a right of entry if the grantor fails to exercise her right within a certain period of time. The doctrine of laches is an equitable doctrine that is based upon the policy that courts aid only those who are vigilant, not those who sleep on their rights. Under the doctrine of laches, after a specified time period has passed following the occurrence of the condition, the grantor may lose her right to divest the grantee of possession. In the above example, if Sam does not exercise his right of entry for several years and the doctrine of laches applies, Sam will be forever barred from exercising his right of entry. As a consequence, Diane's interest then becomes a fee simple absolute (no longer subject to a condition subsequent).

Originally, under the common law, a right of entry was not alienable or devisable. However, in most jurisdictions today, rights of entry are freely alienable, devisable, and inheritable.

Ambiguity in the Conveyance

When a conveyance is ambiguous, the court must decide if the grantor intended to convey: (i) a fee simple determinable; (ii) a fee simple subject to condition subsequent; (iii) a fee simple with a covenant in which the grantee promises the grantor to use the land for a specific purpose; or (iv) an estate in fee simple which merely states an intended use.

Traditionally, the courts look to the intention of the parties to determine which type of estate has been created. Under modern analysis, the fee simple subject to condition subsequent is the preferred estate (over the fee simple determinable) because the fee simple subject to condition subsequent does not automatically cause a forfeiture of the estate. Unlike the fee simple determinable, the fee simple subject to condition subsequent divests the grantee only when the grantor affirmatively acts to reclaim the estate after the condition is broken. This presumption in favor of a fee simple subject to condition subsequent is more favorable to the grantee and more favorable to the modern marketplace since it avoids automatic forfeiture of property.

Often the question before the court is whether the grantor has created any type of defeasible fee at all. The court must look to the method of termination contained in the language of the conveyance to determine the intention of the grantor. When a conveyance does not contain a clause that expressly states that the estate will revert to the grantor, or an explicit re-entry clause, the court must attempt to determine the grantor's intention. The modern trend is to refuse to construe a conveyance as creating an estate on condition subsequent in the absence of a re-entry clause. Today, courts, in their abhorrence of any type of forfeiture, often construe conditional language as a covenant (promise). If the covenant is broken, the grantor's remedy is to sue for damages or injunctive relief. Possession, however, continues.

The Doctrine of Waste

The doctrine of waste concerns the duty of a present possessor to not unduly injure the rights of future interest holders (see Life Estates). This doctrine is usually not applied to defeasible fees and their future interests. Normally, the possibility of the fee being "defeased" is considered as neither reasonably foreseeable nor probable. The interest of the holder of a possibility of reverter or a right of entry is deemed to be too remote an interest for operation of the doctrine of waste.

Fee Simple Defeasible Problems

1.   Sam ➔ Diane and her heirs until Boston becomes a state.

T	
SoT	

2.   Sam ➔ Diane, but if poetry books are sold on the premises, then Sam shall have the right to re-enter and retake the estate.

T	
SoT	

1.　　Sam ➜ Diane and her heirs until Boston becomes a state.

T	Sam to Diane in <u>fee simple</u> **until** (determinable) Boston becomes a state	
SoT	Diane Sam	- fee simple determinable - possibility of reverter

The words of purchase "to Diane" denote Diane as the grantee of the present possessory interest; thus, she receives the estate. The words of limitation "and her heirs" identify the estate as a fee simple. However, the additional word of limitation "until" creates a fee simple determinable, which is a defeasible fee. The estate will automatically end on the occurrence of a specified event. Diane's present interest is a fee simple determinable. She will lose the estate if, and when, Boston becomes a state.

Sam, the grantor, retains a future interest known as a possibility of reverter. The interest becomes possessory automatically upon the happening of the stated event. Sam's future interest will become possessory if Boston becomes a state.

2.　　Sam ➜ Diane, but if poetry books are sold on the premises, then Sam shall have the right to re-enter and retake the estate.

T	Sam to Diane in <u>fee simple</u>, **but if** (subject to condition subsequent) poetry books are sold, then Sam has the right to re-enter and retake the estate	
SoT	Diane Sam	- fee simple subject to condition subsequent - right of entry

The words of purchase "to Diane" denote Diane as the grantee of the present possessory interest; thus, she receives the estate. There are no words of limitation so a fee simple is presumed. However, the additional words of limitation "but if" create a fee simple subject to a condition subsequent, which is a defeasible fee. The estate can be cut short if the express condition is broken. The conveyance also contains words of re-entry, which further manifest the grantor's intent to create a fee simple subject to condition subsequent. Diane has a fee simple subject to condition subsequent. She (or her grantee, devisee or heir) can lose the estate if poetry books are sold on the premises.

Sam, the grantor, retains a future interest known as a right of entry. Upon the happening of the stated event, the grantor has the right to re-enter and reclaim the estate (unlike the fee simple determinable, the estate does not automatically end). The grantor must take affirmative action and exercise this right to regain possession of the estate (and, if limited by the doctrine of laches, must do so within some fixed period of time). The estate of the grantee continues until the grantor exercises the right of entry (power of termination). If anyone sells poetry books on the premises, Sam (or, depending on the jurisdiction, his grantee, devisee, or heir) has the right to re-enter the estate and assert the right to retake possession.

3.   Sam ➔ Diane and her heirs on the condition that poetry books are not sold on the premises.

T	
SoT	

4.   Sam ➔ Diane and her heirs to be used as a bar.

T	
SoT	

3. Sam ➜ Diane and her heirs on the condition that poetry books are not sold on the premises.

T	Sam to Diane in <u>fee simple</u> **on the condition that** (subject to condition subsequent) poetry books are not sold on the premises	
SoT	Diane	- fee simple subject to condition subsequent
	Sam	- right of entry

The words of purchase "to Diane" denote Diane as the grantee of the present possessory interest; thus, she receives the estate. The words of limitation "and her heirs" identify the estate as a fee simple. However, the additional words of limitation "on the condition that" create a fee simple subject to a condition subsequent, which is a defeasible fee. The estate can be cut short if the express condition is broken. Diane has a fee simple subject to a condition subsequent. She (or her grantee, devisee, or heir) can lose the estate if poetry books are sold on the premises.

Sam, the grantor, retains a future interest known as a right of entry. Upon the happening of the stated event, the grantor has the right to re-enter the estate (unlike the fee simple determinable, the estate does not automatically end). The grantor must take affirmative action and exercise this right to regain possession of the estate. The estate of the grantee continues until the grantor exercises the right of entry (power of termination). If anyone sells poetry books on the premises, Sam (or, depending on the jurisdiction, his grantee, devisee, or heir) has the right to re-enter the estate and assert the right to retake possession.

Note, that even though words indicating a right of entry are not expressly used, this right of entry will be presumed.

4. Sam ➜ Diane and her heirs to be used as a bar.

T	Sam to Diane in <u>fee simple</u> to be used as a bar
SoT	Diane - fee simple

The words of purchase "to Diane" denote Diane as the grantee of the present possessory interest; thus, she receives the estate. The words of limitation "and her heirs" identify the estate as a fee simple. Words of divestment are not present in the conveyance; therefore, given the modern presumption in favor of a fee simple, these words would likely be construed to be the rationale or motive for the conveyance, rather than a limitation on the estate.

The grantor retains no future interest because there are no words specifying the estate to be a defeasible fee. Sam does not have the power to gain possession of the premises if the estate is not used as a bar. Diane has a fee simple.

5.   Sam ➔ Diane so long as the estate is not used as a bar.

T	
SoT	

6.   Sam ➔ Diane and her heirs provided that Boston does not become a state, then Sam shall have the right to re-enter and retake the estate.

T	
SoT	

5.   Sam ➜ Diane so long as the estate is not used as a bar.

T	Sam to Diane in <u>fee simple</u> **so long as** (determinable) the estate is not used as a bar
SoT	Diane - fee simple determinable Sam - possibility of reverter

The words of purchase "to Diane" denote Diane as the grantee of the present possessory interest; thus, she receives the estate. There are no words of limitation so a fee simple is presumed. The words of limitation "so long as" create a fee simple determinable, which is a defeasible fee. The estate will automatically end on the occurrence of a specified event. Diane's present interest is a fee simple determinable. She will lose the estate if it is used as a bar.

Sam, the grantor, retains a future interest known as a possibility of reverter. The interest becomes possessory automatically upon the happening of the stated event. Sam's future interest will become possessory if the estate is used as a bar.

6.   Sam ➜ Diane and her heirs provided that Boston does not become a state, then Sam shall have the right to re-enter and retake the estate.

T	Sam to Diane in <u>fee simple</u> **provided that** (subject to a condition subsequent) Boston does not become a state
SoT	Diane - fee simple subject to a condition subsequent Sam - right of entry

The words of purchase "to Diane" denote Diane as the grantee of the present possessory interest; thus, she receives the estate. The words of limitation "and her heirs" identify the estate as a fee simple. However, the additional words of limitation "provided that" create a fee simple subject to a condition subsequent, which is a defeasible fee. The conveyance also includes express words of re-entry which further describe the defeasible fee as a fee simple subject to a condition subsequent. The estate can be cut short if the express condition is broken. Diane has a fee simple subject to a condition subsequent. She (or her grantee, devisee, or heir) can lose the estate if Boston becomes a state.

Sam, the grantor, retains a future interest known as a right of entry. Upon the happening of the stated event, the grantor has the right to re-enter the estate (unlike the fee simple determinable, the estate will not automatically end). The grantor must take affirmative action and exercise this right to regain possession of the estate. The estate of the grantee continues until the grantor exercises the right of entry (power of termination). If Boston becomes a state, Sam (or, depending on the jurisdiction, his grantee, devisee, or heir) has the right to re-enter the estate and assert the right to retake possession.

7.   Sam ➜ Diane and her heirs, but if Sam is alive at Diane's death, then Sam shall have the right to re-enter and retake the estate.

T	
SoT	

8.   Sam ➜ Diane and her heirs as long as Diane does not marry Frazier, but if she does, then Sam shall have the right to re-enter and retake the estate.

T	
SoT	

7.   Sam ➔ Diane and her heirs, but if Sam is alive at Diane's death, then Sam shall have the right to re-enter and retake the estate.

T	Sam to Diane in <u>fee simple</u>, **but if** (subject to a condition subsequent) Sam is alive at Diane's death, then Sam has the right to re-enter and retake possession
SoT	Diane - fee simple subject to a condition subsequent Sam - right of entry

The words of purchase "to Diane" denote Diane as the grantee of the present possessory interest; thus, she receives the estate. The words of limitation "and her heirs" identify the estate as a fee simple. However, the words "but if" create a fee simple subject to a condition subsequent, which is a defeasible fee. The conveyance also includes express words of re-entry which further describe the defeasible fee as a fee simple subject to a condition subsequent. The estate can be cut short on the occurrence of a specified condition. Diane has a fee simple subject to a condition subsequent. She (or her grantee, devisee, or heir) can lose the estate if Sam is alive upon her death and chooses to take possession.

Sam, the grantor, retains a future interest known as a right of entry. Upon the happening of the stated event, the grantor has the right to re-enter the estate (unlike the fee simple determinable, the estate will not automatically end). The grantor must take affirmative action and exercise this right to regain possession of the estate. The estate of the grantee continues until the grantor exercises the right of entry (power of termination). If Sam is alive upon Diane's death, he (or, depending on the jurisdiction, his grantee, devisee, or heir) has the right to re-enter the estate and assert the right to retake possession.

8.   Sam ➔ Diane and her heirs as long as Diane does not marry Frazier, but if she does, then Sam shall have the right to re-enter and retake the estate.

T	Sam to Diane in <u>fee simple</u> **as long as** (determinable) Diane does not marry Frazier, but if she does, then Sam shall have the right to re-enter and take the estate
SoT	Diane - fee simple subject to a condition subsequent Sam - right of entry

The words of purchase "to Diane" denote Diane as the grantee of the present possessory interest; thus, she receives the estate. The words of limitation "and her heirs" identify the estate as a fee simple. However, the additional words of limitation "as long as" seem to create a fee simple determinable, which is a defeasible fee. The conveyance also contains express words of entry that describe a fee simple subject to a condition subsequent. The result is an ambiguous conveyance. When there is an ambiguity, modern law prefers to find a fee simple subject to condition subsequent in order to avoid automatic forfeiture of property. Therefore, the conveyance will be construed as a fee simple subject to a condition subsequent. Diane (or her grantee, devisee, or heir) can lose the estate if she marries Frazier.

Sam, the grantor, retains a future interest known as a right of entry. Upon the happening of the stated event, the grantor has the right to re-enter the estate (unlike the fee simple determinable, the estate will not automatically end). The grantor must take affirmative action and exercise this right to regain possession of the estate. The estate of the grantee continues until the grantor exercises his right of entry (power of termination). If Diane marries Frazier, Sam (or, depending on the jurisdiction, his grantee, devisee, or heir) has the right to re-enter the estate and assert the right to retake possession.

9.   Sam ➔ Diane for life, then to Woody and his heirs so long as the Celtics play basketball.

T	
SoT	

10.   Sam ➔ Diane for life, then to Carla and her heirs so it may be used as a children's home.

T	
SoT	

9.   Sam ➜ Diane for life, then to Woody and his heirs so long as the Celtics play basketball.

T	Sam to Diane in <u>life estate</u>, then to Woody in <u>fee simple</u> **so long as** (determinable) the Celtics play basketball	
SoT	Diane Woody Sam	- life estate - vested remainder in fee simple determinable - possibility of reverter

The words of purchase "to Diane" denote Diane as the grantee of the present possessory interest; thus, she receives the estate. The words of limitation "for life" identify the estate as a life estate.

The words of purchase "to Woody" denote Woody as the grantee of a future interest. The words of limitation "and his heirs" identify the estate as a fee simple. The interest is a remainder because (i) it is capable of becoming possessory immediately upon the expiration of the preceding estate and (ii) it cannot divest any other interests. It is vested because Woody is ascertainable at the time of the conveyance and there is no condition precedent to gaining possession. However, the additional words of limitation "so long as" create a fee simple determinable, which is a defeasible fee. Woody's future interest is a vested remainder in fee simple determinable. He will lose the estate if, and when, the Celtics stop playing basketball.

Sam, the grantor, retains a future interest known as a possibility of reverter. The interest becomes possessory automatically upon the happening of the stated event (assuming Diane is dead). Sam's future interest will become possessory if, and when, the Celtics no longer play basketball.

10.   Sam ➜ Diane for life, then to Carla and her heirs so it may be used as a children's home.

T	Sam to Diane in <u>life estate</u> then to Carla in <u>fee simple</u> so it may be used as a children's home	
SoT	Diane Carla	- life estate - vested remainder in fee simple

The words of purchase "to Diane" denote Diane as the grantee of the present possessory interest; thus, she receives the estate. The words of limitation "for life" identify the estate as a life estate.

The words of purchase "to Carla" denote Carla as the grantee of a future interest. The words of limitation "and her heirs" identify the estate as a fee simple. The interest is a remainder because (i) it is capable of becoming possessory immediately upon the expiration of the preceding estate and (ii) it cannot divest any other interests. It is vested because Carla is ascertainable at the time of the conveyance and there is no condition precedent.

Since no words of divestment are present in the conveyance, a defeasible fee has not been created. The words "so it may be used as a children's home" merely describe the grantor's motive for the conveyance. They do not qualify the duration of the interest or create a future interest in the grantor. Specific words of limitation are needed to create a defeasible fee. Carla's estate will continue indefinitely regardless of whether it is used as a children's home.

III. Future Interests In Transferees

Remainders

Whenever a future interest is created in a grantee (transferee), it is either a remainder or an executory interest.

> A remainder is a future interest in a grantee (transferee) that:
>
> (i) is capable of becoming possessory immediately upon the expiration of the prior estate; and
>
> (ii) cannot divest (cut short) any interest in a prior transferee.

Ex: Oscar ➜ Amy for life, then to Ben.

T	Oscar to Amy in <u>life estate</u>, then to Ben in <u>fee simple</u>
SoT	Amy - life estate Ben - remainder in fee simple

The words of purchase "to Amy" denote Amy as the grantee of the present possessory interest; thus, Amy receives the estate. The words of limitation "for life" identify the estate as a life estate.

The words of purchase "to Ben" denote Ben as the grantee of a future interest. Words of limitation are absent, so a fee simple is presumed. Ben has a remainder because (i) the interest is capable of becoming possessory immediately at the end of Amy's life estate and (ii) it cannot divest (cut short) Amy's life estate. [Ben cannot gain possession before Amy's death; Ben must "wait patiently" for the preceding life estate to naturally end.]

Remainders are freely alienable, inheritable, and devisable. The holder of a remainder can assign that future interest to another person. If Oscar conveys "to Amy for life, then to Ben and his heirs," and Ben dies before Amy, leaving his remainder to his son in his will, then Ben's son receives the remainder and gains the possessory interest when Amy dies. If Ben dies without leaving a will, his remainder will descend to his heirs under the applicable laws of intestate succession. Additionally, Ben can sell his remainder to Carla. Carla then holds the future interest and gets possession when Amy dies.

A remainder must be capable of becoming possessory immediately upon the expiration of the preceding estate

A remainder must be capable of becoming possessory at the termination of the prior estate. No matter how unlikely the probability of that interest becoming possessory, if there is any possibility of its becoming possessory, it can be a remainder.

Ex: Snow White ➜ Doc for life, then to the Evil Queen if the Evil Queen gives birth. (The Evil Queen is 90 years old.)

T	Snow White to Doc in life estate, then to the Evil Queen in fee simple if the Evil Queen gives birth
SoT	Doc - life estate Evil Queen - remainder in fee simple Snow White - reversion

In this example, the Evil Queen has a remainder because: (i) the future interest is capable (even though not likely) of becoming possessory immediately upon the expiration of the preceding estate; and (ii) the Evil Queen's future interest cannot divest (cut short) Doc's life estate. The fact that a 90 year old woman is biologically incapable of bearing children is not controlling. A legal possibility of immediate succession is all that is needed. Therefore, because it is legally possible for the Evil Queen to give birth at, or before, Doc's life estate ends (even though not medically possible – disregarding certain modern scientific advances), she meets the requirement for a remainder. Also, remember that we do not care whether the Evil Queen actually gives birth by the time of Doc's death. The requirement looks solely to possibilities, not to realities.

A remainder cannot divest any preceding estate

Remainders "wait patiently" for the preceding estate to expire before they become possessory. If the future interest divests (cuts short) the preceding estate, it is an executory interest rather than a remainder.

Ex: Snow White ➜ Doc for life, then if the Evil Queen becomes the fairest of them all, to the Evil Queen.

T	Snow White to Doc in <u>life estate</u>, then if the Evil Queen becomes the fairest of them all, to the Evil Queen in <u>fee simple</u>
SoT	Doc - life estate Evil Queen - remainder in fee simple Snow White - reversion

The Evil Queen has a remainder because her interest (i) is capable of becoming possessory immediately upon the expiration of Doc's life estate, and (ii) the Evil Queen cannot divest Doc's interest. Even if the Evil Queen becomes the fairest of them all tomorrow, she must wait until Doc dies before she has the right to possession. Focusing only on the conveyance, there is no way for the Evil Queen to gain her possessory interest any time before Doc's death. She must wait patiently for the life estate to end before coming into possession. She has no power to cut short Doc's life estate.

Ex: Snow White ➜ Doc for life, but if the Evil Queen becomes the fairest of them all, then to the Evil Queen.

T	Snow White to Doc in <u>life estate</u>, **but if** the Evil Queen becomes the fairest of them all, then to the Evil Queen in <u>fee simple</u>
SoT	Doc - life estate defeasible Evil Queen - executory interest in fee simple Snow White - reversion

Here the Evil Queen does not have a remainder. Even though her interest (i) is capable of becoming possessory immediately upon the expiration of Doc's life estate, she (ii) has the capability of divesting Doc of his life estate before he dies. The words "but if" are words of divestment (note, how certain wording leads to dramatically different results) and indicate that, when the Evil Queen becomes the fairest, she gains present possession even if Doc is still alive. The Evil Queen has an executory interest, not a remainder, because her future interest has the possibility of divesting Doc of his life estate if, and when, she becomes the fairest of them all. Since remainders never divest (cut short) the preceding estate, the Evil Queen cannot have a remainder.

Note, the words "but if" are words that, inter alia, often signal divestment.

Remainders Never Follow a Vested Fee Simple

By definition, a remainder cannot follow a vested fee simple. This is a basic rule that must be memorized. Any interest created in a third party following a vested fee simple will be an executory interest. A remainder can only follow an estate of a lesser quantum than a fee simple, such as a fee tail, a life estate, or a term of years.

Ex: Snow White ➔   Doc and his heirs so long as it is used as a farm, then to Grumpy and his heirs.

T	Snow White to Doc in <u>fee simple</u> **so long as** it is used as a farm, then to Grumpy in <u>fee simple</u>
SoT	Doc - fee simple on executory limitation Grumpy - executory interest in fee simple

Grumpy's interest appears to meet the two tests of a remainder: (i) it is capable of becoming possessory immediately upon the expiration of the preceding estate; and (ii) it cannot divest (cut short) the preceding interest [Why? because there are no words of divestment – "but if"]. However, under the common law, the bright-line rule is that a remainder never follows a vested fee. Therefore, Grumpy's interest is classified as an executory interest. [Note that while the words of duration "so long as" often indicate a fee simple determinable, here a fee simple on executory limitation is created because the future interest flows to a third party (Grumpy) rather than being retained by the grantor (Snow White).]

Vested and Contingent Remainders

It is important to be able to distinguish between the two types of remainders, vested and contingent, because of the differing legal significance attached to each.

Vested Remainders

> A remainder is vested if:
>
> (i) it is conveyed to an ascertainable person; <u>and</u>
>
> (ii) it is not subject to a condition precedent (other than the natural termination of the preceding estate).

(i) ascertainable individual

Ascertainable individuals are individuals to whom you can point. At the time of the conveyance, they must exist and must be identifiable. Unborn children or groups of individuals that cannot be identified at the time of the conveyance [e.g., an inter vivos conveyance to one's heirs since one does not have heirs until they die] are not ascertainable.

(ii) no condition precedent

A condition precedent is a condition that must be met before a remainder will vest. A remainder is vested when no further condition need be fulfilled (other than the natural end of the preceding estate) in order for the interest to become possessory.

Ex: Snow White ➜ Doc for life, then to Sleepy and his heirs. (Sleepy is 5 years old.)

T	Snow White to Doc in <u>life estate</u>, then to Sleepy in <u>fee simple</u>
SoT	Doc - life estate Sleepy - vested remainder in fee simple

Sleepy has a remainder because (i) Sleepy's future interest cannot divest the preceding estate, and (ii) Sleepy's interest is capable of becoming immediately possessory upon the expiration of the preceding estate. Sleepy's remainder is vested because: (i) Sleepy is ascertainable [you can point to him] at the time of the conveyance; and (ii) Sleepy's future interest is not subject to any condition precedent. Sleepy will gain possession upon the natural termination of Doc's life estate without anything further being done.

Contingent Remainders

> A remainder is contingent if:
>
>   (i)   it is given to an unascertainable person: <u>or</u>
>
>   (ii) it is subject to a condition precedent.

(i) unascertainable individual

An unascertainable person is a person to whom you cannot point (at the time of the transfer). This includes unborn individuals. The President of the United States in 2050 is an unascertainable individual; currently, you cannot point to her. Likewise, "my first son to become a lawyer" is an unascertainable individual [assume I have no son who is an attorney], even though I may have one son in law school. Presently, I can only point to "my first son in law school"; whether he is the first of my sons to become a lawyer remains uncertain until he passes the bar and is sworn in as an attorney.

Ex: Snow White ➜ Doc for life, then to Doc's widow.

T	Snow White to Doc in <u>life estate</u>, then to Doc's widow in <u>fee simple</u>
SoT	Doc - life estate Doc's widow - contingent remainder in fee simple Snow White - reversion

Doc's widow has a remainder because (i) Doc's widow's future interest cannot divest the preceding estate, and (ii) Doc's widow's interest is capable of becoming possessory immediately upon the expiration of the preceding estate. Doc's widow has a contingent remainder because Doc's widow is unascertainable until Doc's death. [Even though Doc may be presently married, he could divorce this spouse before his death and remarry someone else.] His widow will become ascertainable, and the interest will vest, only upon his death. [Note that Snow White has a reversion in fee simple in case the contingent remainder does not vest.]

(ii) condition precedent

A condition precedent is an express condition that must be fulfilled for the remainder to vest. So long as the condition remains unsatisfied, the remainder individual has no right to immediate possession, even if the preceding estate should come to an end.

Ex: Snow White ➔ Doc for life, then to the Evil Queen and her heirs if she marries.

T	Snow White to Doc in <u>life estate</u>, then to the Evil Queen in <u>fee simple</u> if she marries
SoT	Doc - life estate Evil Queen - contingent remainder in fee simple Snow White - reversion

The Evil Queen has a remainder because (i) it is capable of becoming possessory immediately upon the expiration of Doc's life estate and (ii) it cannot divest Doc's life estate. The remainder is contingent because the Evil Queen must marry before the interest will vest. If the Evil Queen never marries, she cannot gain possession of the parcel, even though Doc has died.

Reversion in the Grantor

A reversion will always follow a contingent remainder because someone must hold seisin in the estate at all times. Seisin means that someone has possession of the land under claim of a freehold estate. Since contingent remainders are not certain to vest, the grantor always retains a reversion. In the event that the condition precedent is not fulfilled or the person never becomes ascertainable, the estate reverts to the grantor. There is no gap in seisin.

Alternative Contingent Remainders

A grantor can create alternative contingent remainders. When conveying alternative contingent remainders, the grantor provides that if the condition for vesting is not fulfilled then the estate shall vest in another grantee. One alternative contingent remainder may not divest another. Each "waits patiently" for possession, but only one gains it. Therefore, if one alternative contingent remainder vests, the other cannot. A contingent remainder followed by a "but if" clause generally signals alternative contingent remainders.

Even though alternative contingent remainders are mutually exclusive and will exhaust all possibilities, the grantor is still deemed to have a reversion. Since at common law contingent remainders were destructible, a reversion was necessary so that someone would necessarily be seised at all times of the estate.

Ex: Snow White ➔   Doc for life, then to Dopey and his heirs if Dopey becomes a lawyer, but if not, then to Happy and his heirs.

T	Snow White to Doc in <u>life estate</u>, then to Dopey in <u>fee simple</u> if Dopey becomes a lawyer, but if not, then to Happy in <u>fee simple</u>
SoT	Doc - life estate Dopey - alternative contingent remainder in fee simple Happy - alternative contingent remainder in fee simple Snow White - reversion

Both Dopey and Happy have remainders in fee simple because (i) their interests are capable of becoming possessory immediately upon the expiration of Doc's life estate and (ii) they cannot divest Doc's life estate. The remainders are in fee simple because of the words of limitation "and his heirs." The remainders are contingent because, for Dopey's interest to vest, Dopey must become a lawyer; for Happy's interest to vest, Dopey must die before he becomes a lawyer. Happy's interest will vest only if Dopey's does not. Therefore, they are alternative contingent remainders. Snow White retains a future interest known as a reversion. Even though alternative contingent remainders are mutually exclusive and will exhaust all possibilities, the grantor is still deemed to retain a reversion.

Remainder Problems

1. Snow White ➔ Doc for life, then to Sneezy and his heirs.

T	
SoT	

2. Snow White ➔ Grumpy for life, then to Sleepy and his heirs if Sleepy lives to be 100.

T	
SoT	

1.   Snow White ➔ Doc for life, then to Sneezy and his heirs.

T	Snow White to Doc in <u>life estate</u>, then to Sneezy in <u>fee simple</u>	
SoT	Doc	- life estate
	Sneezy	- vested remainder in fee simple

The words of purchase "to Doc" denote Doc as the grantee of the present possessory interest; thus, he receives the estate. The words of limitation "for life" identify the estate as a life estate.

The words of purchase "to Sneezy" denote Sneezy as the grantee of a future interest. The words of limitation "and his heirs" identify the estate (that will exist when the future interest becomes possessory) as a fee simple. The interest is a remainder because (i) it is capable of becoming possessory immediately upon the expiration of the preceding estate and (ii) it cannot divest any other interests. It is vested because Sneezy is (i) ascertainable at the time of the conveyance [you can point to him] and (ii) there is no condition precedent.

2.   Snow White ➔ Grumpy for life, then to Sleepy and his heirs if Sleepy lives to be 100.

T	Snow White to Grumpy in <u>life estate</u>, then to Sleepy in <u>fee simple</u> if Sleepy lives to be 100	
SoT	Grumpy	- life estate
	Sleepy	- contingent remainder in fee simple
	Snow White	- reversion

The words of purchase "to Grumpy" denote Grumpy as the grantee of the present possessory interest; thus, he receives the estate. The words of limitation "for life" identify the estate as a life estate.

The words of purchase "to Sleepy" denote Sleepy as the grantee of a future interest. The words of limitation "and his heirs" identify the estate (that will exist when the future interest becomes possessory) as a fee simple. The interest is a remainder because (i) it is capable of becoming possessory immediately upon the expiration of the preceding estate and (ii) it cannot divest any other interests. It is a contingent remainder because it is subject to the condition precedent that Sleepy lives to be 100 years old.

Snow White holds a future interest known as a reversion. A reversion will always follow a contingent remainder because someone must hold seisin in the estate at all times. Since a contingent remainder is not certain to vest, the grantor must retain a reversion.

3.   Snow White ➜   Doc for life, then to Bashful for life if Bashful gets married, then to Happy and his heirs.

T	
SoT	

4.   Snow White ➜ Grumpy for 15 years, then to Dopey and his heirs.

T	
SoT	

3. Snow White ➜ Doc for life, then to Bashful for life if Bashful gets married, then to Happy and his heirs.

T	Snow White to Doc in <u>life estate</u>, then to Bashful in <u>life estate</u> if Bashful gets married, then to Happy in <u>fee simple</u>	
SoT	Doc	- life estate
	Bashful	- contingent remainder in life estate
	Happy	- vested remainder in fee simple

The words of purchase "to Doc" denote Doc as the grantee of the present possessory interest; thus, he receives the estate. The words of limitation "for life" identify the estate as a life estate.

The words of purchase "to Bashful" denote Bashful as the grantee of a future interest. The words of limitation "for life" identify the estate (that will exist when the future interest becomes possessory) as a life estate. The interest is a remainder because (i) it is capable of becoming possessory immediately upon the expiration of the preceding estate and (ii) it cannot divest any other interests. It is a contingent remainder because it is subject to the condition precedent that Bashful gets married.

The words of purchase "to Happy" denote Happy as the grantee of a future interest. The words of limitation "and his heirs" identify the estate (that will exist when the future interest becomes possessory) as a fee simple. The interest is a remainder because (i) it is capable of becoming possessory immediately upon the expiration of the preceding estate and (ii) it cannot divest any other interests. It is vested because (i) Happy is ascertainable at the time of the conveyance [you can point to him] and (ii) there is no condition precedent.

4. Snow White ➜ Grumpy for 15 years, then to Dopey and his heirs.

T	Snow White to Grumpy for <u>a term of years</u>, then to Dopey in <u>fee simple</u>	
SoT	Grumpy	- term of years
	Dopey	- vested remainder in fee simple

The words of purchase "to Grumpy" denote Grumpy as the grantee of the present possessory interest; thus, he receives the estate. The words of limitation "for 15 years" identify the estate as a term of years, which is an estate of fixed duration lasting exactly 15 years.

The words of purchase "to Dopey" denote Dopey as the grantee of a future interest. The words of limitation "and his heirs" identify the estate (that will exist when the future interest becomes possessory) as a fee simple. Dopey's future interest is a remainder because (i) it is capable of becoming possessory immediately upon the expiration of the preceding estate and (ii) it cannot divest any other interests. It is vested because (i) Dopey is ascertainable at the time of the conveyance [you can point to him] and (ii) there is no condition precedent.

5.   Snow White ➜ Doc for life, then to Doc's heirs.

T	
SoT	

6.   Snow White ➜ Doc for life, then to Sleepy and the heirs of his body.

T	
SoT	

5.   Snow White ➔ Doc for life, then to Doc's heirs.

T	Snow White to Doc in <u>life estate</u>, then to Doc's heirs in <u>fee simple</u>	
SoT	Doc Doc's heirs Snow White	- life estate - contingent remainder in fee simple - reversion

The words of purchase "to Doc" denote Doc as the grantee of the present possessory interest; thus, he receives the estate. The words of limitation "for life" identify the estate as a life estate.

The words of purchase "to Doc's heirs" denote Doc's heirs as the grantee(s) of a future interest. There are no words of limitation, so a fee simple is presumed. The interest is a remainder because (i) it is capable of becoming possessory immediately upon the expiration of the preceding estate and (ii) it cannot divest any other interests. It is a contingent remainder because, at the time of the conveyance, Doc's heirs are unascertainable [Doc only has heirs at the time of his death; during Doc's life, you cannot point to them].

Snow White retains a future interest known as a reversion. A reversion will follow a contingent remainder because someone must hold seisin in the estate at all times. Since contingent remainders are not certain to vest, the grantor must retain a reversion.

[Note: The Rule in Shelley's Case may apply to this conveyance.]

6.   Snow White ➔ Doc for life, then to Sleepy and the heirs of his body.

T	Snow White to Doc in <u>life estate</u>, then to Sleepy in <u>fee tail</u>	
SoT	Doc Sleepy Snow White	- life estate - vested remainder in fee tail - reversion

The words of purchase "to Doc" denote Doc as the grantee of the present possessory interest; thus, he receives the estate. The words of limitation "for life" identify the estate as a life estate.

The words of purchase "to Sleepy" denote Sleepy as the grantee of a future interest. The words of limitation "and the heirs of his body" identify the estate (that will exist when the future interest becomes possessory) as a fee tail. The interest is a remainder because (i) it is capable of becoming possessory immediately upon the expiration of the preceding estate and (ii) it cannot divest any other interests. It is vested because (i) Sleepy is ascertainable at the time of the conveyance [you can point to him] and (ii) there is no condition precedent.

Since Sleepy's estate is in fee tail, Snow White holds a future interest known as a reversion. Following Doc's life estate, Snow White's reversion will become possessory if, and when, Sleepy's line of descendants ends.

7.   Snow White ➜ Grumpy for life, then to Happy and his heirs if Happy becomes a
                     knight, but if Happy does not become a knight, then to Prince
                     Charming and his heirs.

T	
SoT	

7.   Snow White ➜   Grumpy for life, then to Happy and his heirs if Happy becomes a
                      knight, but if Happy does not become a knight, then to Prince
                      Charming and his heirs.

T	Snow White to Grumpy in <u>life estate</u>, then to Happy in <u>fee simple</u> if he becomes a Knight, **but if** Happy does not become a Knight, then to Prince Charming in <u>fee simple</u>
SoT	Grumpy - life estate Happy - alternative contingent remainder in fee simple Prince Charming - alternative contingent remainder in fee simple Snow White - reversion

The words of purchase "to Grumpy" denote Grumpy as the grantee of the present possessory interest; thus, he receives the estate. The words of limitation "for life" identify the estate as a life estate.

The words of purchase "to Happy" denote Happy as the grantee of a future interest. The words of limitation "and his heirs" identify the estate (that will exist when the future interest becomes possessory) as a fee simple. The interest is a remainder because (i) it is capable of becoming possessory immediately upon the expiration of the preceding estate and (ii) it cannot divest any other interest. It is a contingent remainder because it is subject to the condition precedent that Happy becomes a knight. The interest is an alternative contingent remainder because if the condition for vesting is not fulfilled by one grantee, the interest will vest in another grantee. If one remainder vests, the other cannot. Happy's interest will vest and become possessory if he becomes a knight. If Happy does not become a knight, Prince Charming's interest will vest.

The words of purchase "to Prince Charming" denote Prince Charming as the grantee of a future interest. The words of limitation "and his heirs" identify the estate (that will exist when the future interest becomes possessory) as a fee simple. The interest is a remainder because (i) it is capable of becoming possessory immediately upon the expiration of the preceding estate and (ii) it cannot divest any other interests. It is a contingent remainder because it is subject to the condition precedent that Happy does not become a knight. The interest is an alternative contingent remainder because if the condition for vesting is not fulfilled by one grantee, the interest will vest in another grantee. If one remainder vests, the other cannot. Prince Charming's interest will vest only if Happy's interest does not vest.

Snow White retains a future interest known as a reversion. A reversion will always follow a contingent remainder because someone must hold seisin in the estate at all times. Even though alternative contingent remainders are mutually exclusive and will exhaust all possibilities, the grantor is still deemed to retain a reversion. [In feudal times under certain circumstances, contingent remainders could be forfeited to the king.]

8.   Snow White ➔ Sleepy for life, then to Dopey and his heirs, but if Dopey doesn't use it
                     as a school for gifted children, then to Doc and his heirs.

T	
SoT	

9.   Snow White ➔ Doc for life, then to Grumpy for life, then to Sleepy and his heirs.

T	
SoT	

8.   Snow White ➔   Sleepy for life, then to Dopey and his heirs, but if Dopey doesn't use it
                        as a school for gifted children, then to Doc and his heirs.

T	Snow White to Sleepy in <u>life estate</u>, then to Dopey in <u>fee simple</u>, **but if** Dopey doesn't use it as a school for gifted children, then to Doc in <u>fee simple</u>	
SoT	Sleepy	- life estate
	Dopey	- vested remainder in fee simple on executory limitation
	Doc	- shifting executory interest in fee simple

The words of purchase "to Sleepy" denote Sleepy as the grantee of the present possessory interest; thus, he receives the estate. The words of limitation "for life" identify the estate as a life estate.

The words of purchase "to Dopey" denote Dopey as the grantee of a future interest. The words of limitation "and his heirs" identify the estate (that will exist if the future interest becomes possessory) as a fee simple. The interest is a remainder because (i) it is capable of becoming possessory immediately upon the expiration of the preceding estate and (ii) it cannot divest any other interests. It is vested because (i) Dopey is ascertainable at the time of the conveyance [you can point to him] and (ii) there is no condition precedent. However, the additional words of limitation "but if" are words which create a fee simple defeasible. Since the fee is followed by a flow to a third party, Dopey's interest is a vested remainder in fee simple on executory limitation. Dopey loses possession of the estate if he does not use the property as a school for gifted children.

The words of purchase "to Doc" denote Doc as the grantee of a future interest. The words of limitation "and his heirs" identify the estate (that will exist if the future interest becomes possessory) as a fee simple. Since Dopey's defeasible fee is followed by a flow to a third party, Doc's interest is an executory interest. It is a shifting interest because Doc, a transferee, will divest Dopey, another transferee, of the estate.

9.   Snow White ➔ Doc for life, then to Grumpy for life, then to Sleepy and his heirs.

T	Snow White to Doc in <u>life estate</u>, then to Grumpy in <u>life estate</u>, then to Sleepy in <u>fee simple</u>	
SoT	Doc	-life estate
	Grumpy	-vested remainder in life estate
	Sleepy	- vested remainder in fee simple

The words of purchase "to Doc" denote Doc as the grantee of the present possessory interest; thus, he receives the estate. The words of limitation "for life" identify the estate as a life estate.

The words of purchase "to Grumpy" denote Grumpy as the grantee of a future interest. The words of limitation "for life" identify the estate (that will exist if the future interest becomes possessory) as a life estate. The interest is a remainder because (i) it is capable of becoming possessory immediately upon the expiration of the preceding estate and (ii) it cannot divest any other interests. It is vested because (i) Grumpy is ascertainable at the time of the conveyance [you can point to him] and (ii) there is no condition precedent.

The words of purchase "to Sleepy" denote Sleepy as the grantee of a future interest. The words of limitation "and his heirs" identify the estate (that will exist if the future interest becomes possessory) as a fee simple. The interest is a remainder because (i) it is capable of becoming possessory immediately upon the expiration of the preceding estate and (ii) it cannot divest any other interests. It is vested because (i) Sleepy is ascertainable at the time of the conveyance [you can point to him] and (ii) there is no condition precedent.

10.   Snow White ➔   Grumpy for life, then to Bashful for life if Bashful marries, then to
                        Bashful's first child to reach 21 and his heirs.

        Facts: Bashful is unmarried and has no children.

T	
SoT	

10.   Snow White ➔   Grumpy for life, then to Bashful for life if Bashful marries, then to Bashful's first child to reach 21 and his heirs.

Facts: Bashful is unmarried and has no children.

T	Snow White to Grumpy in <u>life estate</u>, then to Bashful in <u>life estate</u> if Bashful marries, then to Bashful's first child to reach 21 in <u>fee simple</u>	
SoT	Grumpy Bashful First child to reach 21 Snow White	- life estate - contingent remainder in life estate - contingent remainder in fee simple - reversion

The words of purchase "to Grumpy" denote Grumpy as the grantee of the present possessory interest; thus, he receives the estate. The words of limitation "for life" identify the estate as a life estate.

The words of purchase "to Bashful" denote Bashful as the grantee of a future interest. The words of limitation "for life" identify the estate (that will exist if the future interest becomes possessory) as a life estate. The interest is a remainder because (i) it is capable of becoming possessory immediately upon the expiration of the preceding estate and (ii) it cannot divest any other interests. It is a contingent remainder because it is subject to the condition precedent that Bashful marry (before his interest will vest).

The words of purchase "to Bashful's first child to reach 21" denote the grantee of a future interest. The words of limitation "and his heirs" identify the estate (that will exist if the future interest becomes possessory) as a fee simple. The future interest is a remainder because (i) it is capable of becoming possessory immediately upon the expiration of the preceding estate and (ii) it cannot divest any other interests. It is a contingent remainder because, at the time of the conveyance, "Bashful's first child to reach 21" is not yet ascertainable since Bashful has no children (thus, you cannot point to her). [Even if Bashful had ten children (none of whom were 21 at the time of the conveyance), the remainder would still be contingent as the grantee is identified as "the first of Bashful's children to reach 21"; not the first child of Bashful.] Note, these are not alternative contingent remainders as both interests are capable of vesting.

Snow White retains a future interest known as a reversion. A reversion will always follow a contingent remainder because someone must hold seisin in the estate at all times. Since a contingent remainder is not certain to vest, the grantor must retain a reversion.

Executory Interests

An executory interest is one of two types of future interests created in a transferee (grantee); a remainder is the other. An executory interest is a future interest that either (i) divests the preceding estate upon the occurrence or non-occurrence of a stated condition, or (ii) is incapable of becoming possessory immediately upon the expiration of the preceding estate. In order to become possessory, an executory interest must divest an interest in either the transferee or the transferor. When a transferee is divested, the interest is labeled a shifting executory interest. When the transferor is divested, the interest is labeled a springing executory interest.

Ex: Gilligan ➔ Ginger for life, then one year after Ginger dies, to Maryanne and her heirs.

T	Gilligan to Ginger in <u>life estate</u>, then one year after Ginger dies, to Maryanne in <u>fee simple</u>
SoT	Ginger - life estate Maryanne - springing executory interest in fee simple Gilligan - reversion in fee simple on executory limitation

The words of purchase "to Ginger" denote Ginger as the grantee of the present possessory interest; thus, she receives the estate. The words of limitation "for life" identify the estate as a life estate. The words "one year after Ginger dies" create a gap in the possession between Ginger's life estate and Maryanne's fee simple. Because someone must hold seisin in the estate at all times, during the one-year gap, Gilligan will regain possession of the estate. After the expiration of that year, Maryanne's interest will become possessory. Thus, Gilligan has a reversion (a future interest in the grantor) in fee simple on executory limitation (a defeasible fee that is followed by an interest in a third party), and Maryanne has a springing executory interest (her interest follows the grantor's).

An executory interest is a non-vested interest. An executory interest is regarded as vested only when it becomes possessory.

When an interest is created in a third party following a defeasible fee simple, common law rules dictate that the future interest can only be an executory interest (rather than a remainder). The defeasible fee is called a fee simple on executory limitation (it is also referred to as a fee simple subject to divestment).

An executory interest is alienable, inheritable, and devisable.

Shifting and Springing Interests

A shifting executory interest is one that divests the interest of another transferee. It will always cut short a prior estate created by the same conveyance.

Ex: Gilligan ➔ Ginger and her heirs, but if Ginger leaves the island, then to Maryanne and her heirs.

T	Gilligan to Ginger in <u>fee simple</u>, but if Ginger leaves the island, then to Maryanne in <u>fee simple</u>
SoT	Ginger - fee simple on executory limitation Maryanne - shifting executory interest in fee simple

The words of purchase "to Ginger" denote Ginger as the grantee of a possessory interest. The words of limitation "and her heirs" create a fee simple. The words "but if" (following a vested fee simple) indicate a defeasible fee. Since Ginger's defeasible fee is followed by a future interest in Maryanne (rather than in the grantor, Gilligan), an executory interest is created. Ginger holds a fee simple on executory limitation [also called a fee simple subject to divestment]. Maryanne has a shifting executory interest in fee simple. It is a shifting interest because Maryanne, a transferee, will divest Ginger, another transferee, of the estate [when, and if, Ginger leaves the island].

A springing executory interest is a future interest that divests the transferor (grantor) of the estate, following a gap in possession. When the executory interest follows a gap in possession between transferees, it springs out of the transferor's reversion. When the transferor retains present possession, the executory interest will spring out of the transferor's (grantor's) fee.

Ex: Gilligan ➔ Ginger when Ginger marries Professor.

T	Gilligan to Ginger in <u>fee simple</u> when Ginger marries Professor	
SoT	Gilligan	- fee simple on executory limitation
	Ginger	- springing executory interest in fee simple

Gilligan retains present possession of the fee simple estate until Ginger marries Professor. Since Ginger will divest Gilligan of his estate, Gilligan has the present estate, labeled a fee simple on executory limitation [also called a fee simple subject to divestment.]

Ginger has an executory interest in fee simple because she may divest the preceding estate. It is a springing interest because Ginger, the transferee, will divest Gilligan, the transferor, of the estate.

Remember the rule: a remainder can never follow a vested fee simple. This rule applies to both examples above and is an easy explanation of why the future interests in each case are labeled as executory interests.

Executory Interest Problems

1. Gilligan ➜ The City of Sacramento, its successors and assigns, but if the land is not used as a historical site, then to Ginger and her heirs.

T	
SoT	

2. Gilligan ➜ Skipper and his heirs upon the first anniversary of Skipper's marriage.

T	
SoT	

1.   Gilligan ➔ The City of Sacramento, its successors and assigns, but if the land is not
                used as a historical site, then to Ginger and her heirs.

T	Gilligan to the City of Sacramento in <u>fee simple</u>, **but if** the land is not used as a historical site, then to Ginger in <u>fee simple</u>
SoT	Sacramento - fee simple on executory limitation Ginger - shifting executory interest in fee simple

The words of purchase "to the City of Sacramento" denote the City as the grantee of the present possessory interest; thus, the City receives the estate. The words of limitation "its successors and assigns" identify the estate as a fee simple (note, entities do not have "heirs," rather they have "successors and assigns"). However, the words "but if" create a fee simple subject to a condition subsequent, which is a defeasible fee. The estate can be cut short on the occurrence of a specified condition. Since the City's defeasible fee simple is followed by a future interest in a third party, the City of Sacramento has a fee simple on executory limitation.

The words of purchase "to Ginger" denote Ginger as the grantee of a future interest. The words of limitation "and her heirs" identify the future interest (that will exist when the future interest becomes possessory) as a fee simple. Since a future interest in a third party follows a defeasible fee, Ginger's future interest is an executory interest (because she is a third party and not the grantor). It is a shifting interest because Ginger, a transferee, may divest the City, another transferee, of the estate if the land is not used as a historical site. [Note: The Rule Against Perpetuities may affect this conveyance.]

2.   Gilligan ➔ Skipper and his heirs upon the first anniversary of Skipper's marriage.

T	Gilligan to Skipper in <u>fee simple</u> upon the first anniversary of Skipper's marriage
SoT	Gilligan - fee simple on executory limitation Skipper - springing executory interest in fee simple

The words of purchase "to Skipper" denote Skipper as the grantee of an interest. The words of limitation "and his heirs" identify the estate (that will exist when the future interest becomes possessory) as a fee simple. Skipper does not have present possession because the conveyance states a condition which must occur prior to Skipper gaining possession of the fee; therefore, Skipper's interest is a future interest. Skipper's future interest is not a remainder because a remainder can never follow a vested fee simple estate. It is a springing interest because Skipper, the transferee, will divest Gilligan, the transferor, of the estate.

Gilligan retains present possession of the estate. He holds a fee simple on executory limitation (subject to divestment). His interest will be cut short if Skipper celebrates his first wedding anniversary. Since Skipper will divest Gilligan of his estate, Gilligan has a fee simple on executory limitation.

3.   Gilligan ➜ the City of Sacramento, its successors and assigns, so long as it is used as a historical site.

T	
SoT	

4.   Gilligan ➜ Skipper for life, then to Ginger and her heirs.

T	
SoT	

3.   Gilligan ➜ the City of Sacramento, its successors and assigns, so long as it is used as a historical site.

T	Gilligan to the City of Sacramento in <u>fee simple</u> **so long as** it is used as a historical site
SoT	Sacramento - fee simple determinable Gilligan - possibility of reverter

The words of purchase "to the City of Sacramento" denote the City as the grantee of the present possessory interest; thus, the City receives the estate. The words of limitation "its successors and assigns" identify the estate as a fee simple. However, the words "so long as" create a fee simple determinable, which is a defeasible fee. The City will lose the estate if the land is not used as a historical site.

Gilligan, the grantor, retains a future interest known as a possibility of reverter. The interest becomes possessory automatically upon the happening of the stated event. Gilligan's future interest will become possessory if the City fails to use the property as a historical site. This is not an executory interest because the defeasible fee is not followed by a future interest in a third party. [Note: The Rule Against Perpetuities may affect this conveyance.]

4.   Gilligan ➜ Skipper for life, then to Ginger and her heirs.

T	Gilligan to Skipper in <u>life estate</u>, then to Ginger in <u>fee simple</u>
SoT	Skipper - life estate Ginger - vested remainder in fee simple

The words of purchase "to Skipper" denote Skipper as the grantee of the present possessory interest; thus, he receives the estate. The words of limitation "for life" identify the estate as a life estate.

The words of purchase "to Ginger" denote Ginger as the grantee of a future interest. The words of limitation "and her heirs" identify the estate (that will exist when the future interest becomes possessory) as a fee simple. The interest is a remainder because (i) it is capable of becoming possessory immediately upon the expiration of the preceding estate and (ii) it cannot divest any other interests. It is vested because Ginger is (i) ascertainable at the time of the conveyance and (ii) there is no condition precedent.

No executory interest is created because the future interest in a third party does not divest the present possessory estate. Ginger's future interest becomes possessory only upon the natural termination of the preceding estate. Ginger must wait patiently for Skipper's life estate to end.

5.   Gilligan ➔ Skipper for life.

T	
SoT	

Gilligan ➔   Professor "all interest that I have in the estate which I have given to Skipper for his life."

T	
SoT	

6.   Gilligan ➔   Skipper and his heirs so long as the forest is left pristine; otherwise, to Ginger and her heirs.

T	
SoT	

5. Gilligan ➔ Skipper for life.

T	Gilligan to Skipper in <u>life estate</u>
SoT	Skipper — - life estate Gilligan — - reversion

Gilligan ➔ Professor "all interest that I have in the estate which I have given to Skipper for his life."

T	Gilligan to Professor in <u>fee simple</u>
SoT	Professor — - reversion

The words of purchase "to Skipper" denote Skipper as the grantee of the present possessory interest in the first conveyance; thus, he receives the estate. The words of limitation "for life" identify the estate as a life estate. In the first conveyance, since Gilligan carved out a smaller estate from his larger estate, he retains a reversion which will become possessory upon the expiration of the life estate. Gilligan (or his grantee, devisee, or heir) will gain possession of the estate at the death of Skipper.

In the second conveyance, the words of purchase "to Professor" denote Professor as the grantee of an interest. There are no words of limitation, so a fee simple is presumed. At the time of the second conveyance, Gilligan's interest in the property is a reversion. Reversions are alienable, devisable, and inheritable. Since Gilligan can convey his reversion, Professor will receive Gilligan's reversion. Professor's interest becomes possessory at the expiration of Skipper's life estate. Gilligan retains nothing.

No executory interest is created because the present possessory interest is not being divested by the future interest. Professor's future interest will become possessory upon the natural termination of Skipper's life estate. Professor must wait patiently for Skipper's life estate to end.

6. Gilligan ➔ Skipper and his heirs so long as the forest is left pristine; otherwise, to Ginger and her heirs.

T	Gilligan to Skipper in <u>fee simple</u>, **so long as** the forest is left pristine; otherwise, to Ginger in <u>fee simple</u>
SoT	Skipper — - fee simple on executory limitation Ginger — - shifting executory interest

The words of purchase "to Skipper" denote Skipper as the grantee of the present possessory interest; thus, he receives the estate. The words of limitation "and his heirs" identify the estate as a fee simple. However, the words "so long as" are words of divestment that create a defeasible fee. Since Skipper's defeasible fee simple is followed by a future interest in a third party, Skipper has a fee simple on executory limitation.

The words of purchase "to Ginger" denote Ginger as the grantee of a future interest. The words of limitation "and her heirs" identify the estate (that will exist when the future interest becomes possessory) as a fee simple. Since Ginger's future interest follows a defeasible fee, it is an executory interest. It is a shifting interest because Ginger, a transferee, will divest Skipper, another transferee, of the estate.

[Note: The Rule Against Perpetuities may affect this conveyance.]

7.   Gilligan ➔ Maryanne for life, then to Professor and his heirs, but if Professor dies without issue, then to Thurston and his heirs.

T	
SoT	

8.   Gilligan ➔ Skipper for life, then to Maryanne and her heirs after she gives Skipper a decent burial.

T	
SoT	

7.   Gilligan ➜ Maryanne for life, then to Professor and his heirs, but if Professor dies without issue, then to Thurston and his heirs.

T	Gilligan to Maryanne in <u>life estate</u>, then to Professor in <u>fee simple</u>, **but if** Professor dies without issue, then to Thurston in <u>fee simple</u>
SoT	Maryanne - life estate Professor - vested remainder in fee simple on executory limitation Thurston - shifting executory interest in fee simple

The words of purchase "to Maryanne" denote Maryanne as the grantee of the present possessory interest; thus, she receives the estate. The words of limitation "for life" identify the estate as a life estate.

The words of purchase "to Professor" denote Professor as the grantee of a future interest. The words of limitation "and his heirs" identify the estate (that will exist when the future interest becomes possessory) as a fee simple. The interest is a remainder because (i) it is capable of becoming possessory immediately upon the expiration of the preceding estate and (ii) it cannot divest any other interests. It is vested because Professor is (i) ascertainable at the time of the conveyance and (ii) there is no condition precedent. However, the words "but if" are words of limitation that create a defeasible fee. Since Professor's defeasible fee simple interest is followed by a future interest in a third party, Professor has a vested remainder in fee simple on executory limitation.

The words of purchase "to Thurston" denote Thurston as the grantee of a future interest. The words of limitation "and his heirs" identify the estate (that will exist when the future interest becomes possessory) as a fee simple. Since Professor's defeasible fee simple is followed by a future interest in a third party, Thurston's interest is an executory interest. It is a shifting interest because Thurston, a transferee, will divest Professor, another transferee, of the estate.

[Note: The Rule Against Perpetuities may affect this conveyance.]

8.   Gilligan ➜ Skipper for life, then to Maryanne and her heirs after she gives Skipper a decent burial.

T	Gilligan to Skipper in <u>life estate</u>, then to Maryanne in <u>fee simple</u> after she gives Skipper a decent burial
SoT	Skipper - life estate Gilligan - reversion in fee simple on executory limitation Maryanne - springing executory interest in fee simple

The words of purchase "to Skipper" denote Skipper as the grantee of the present possessory interest; thus, he receives the estate. The words of limitation "for life" identify the estate as a life estate.

The words of purchase "to Maryanne" denote Maryanne as the grantee of a future interest. The words of limitation "and her heirs" identify the estate (that will exist when the future interest becomes possessory) as a fee simple. However, the conveyance states a condition which must occur prior to Maryanne gaining possession of the fee; therefore, Maryanne's interest is a future interest. Since there will necessarily be a gap in time between Skipper's death and his burial (regardless of how short that time might be), Gilligan retains a reversion on executory limitation because someone must hold seisin in the estate at all times. Thus, Maryanne has an executory interest in fee simple that will become possessory after Skipper's burial. It is a springing interest because Maryanne, a transferee, will divest Gilligan, the transferor, of the estate.

9. Gilligan ➜ Skipper and his heirs, but if Ginger marries, then to Ginger and her heirs.

T	
SoT	

10. Gilligan ➜ Skipper for life, then one year after Skipper's death, to Ginger and her heirs.

T	
SoT	

9.   Gilligan ➜ Skipper and his heirs, but if Ginger marries, then to Ginger and her heirs.

T	Gilligan to Skipper in <u>fee simple</u>, **but if** Ginger marries, then to Ginger in <u>fee simple</u>
SoT	Skipper - fee simple on executory limitation Ginger - shifting executory interest in fee simple

The words of purchase "to Skipper" denote Skipper as the grantee of the present possessory interest; thus, he receives the estate. The words of limitation "and his heirs" identify the estate as a fee simple. The words "but if" are words of limitation that create a defeasible fee. Skipper's interest will be cut short if the specified condition is met. Since Skipper's defeasible fee is followed by a future interest in a third party, Skipper has a fee simple on executory limitation.

The words of purchase "to Ginger" denote Ginger as the grantee of a future interest. The words of limitation "and her heirs" identify the estate (that will exist if the future interest becomes possessory) as a fee simple. Since a future interest in a third party follows a defeasible fee, Ginger's future interest is an executory interest. It is a shifting interest because Ginger, a transferee, will divest Skipper, another transferee, of the estate.

10.   Gilligan ➜ Skipper for life, then one year after Skipper's death, to Ginger and her heirs.

T	Gilligan to Skipper in <u>life estate</u>, then one year later to Ginger in <u>fee simple</u>
SoT	Skipper - life estate Gilligan - reversion in fee simple on executory limitation Ginger - springing executory interest in fee simple

The words of purchase "to Skipper" denote Skipper as the grantee of the present possessory interest; thus, he receives the estate. The words of limitation "for life" identify the estate as a life estate.

The words of purchase "to Ginger" denote Ginger as the grantee of a future interest. The words of limitation "and her heirs" identify the estate (that will exist when the future interest becomes possessory) as a fee simple. Ginger's future interest is not a remainder because it will not become possessory immediately upon the expiration of the preceding estate. Therefore, her future interest is an executory interest in fee simple. It is a springing interest because Ginger, the transferee, will divest Gilligan, the transferor, of the estate.

Gilligan holds a future interest known as a reversion in fee simple on executory limitation; it becomes possessory upon the expiration of Skipper's life estate. At all times someone must hold seisin in the estate. Since Ginger's interest does not become possessory until one year after the end of Skipper's life estate, the possessory interest reverts to Gilligan, who is seised of the estate for the one year period between Skipper's and Ginger's estates. Gilligan holds the estate in fee simple. Since Ginger's interest cannot become immediately possessory upon the expiration of the preceding estate of Skipper, Gilligan has a reversion in fee simple on executory limitation.

IV. Rules Furthering Marketability

Rule in Shelley's Case

The Rule in Shelley's Case (also known as Shelley's Rule or the Rule Against Remainders in Grantee's Heirs) furthers marketability. It was originally developed to protect the rights of the feudal lords by taking the remainder away from the grantee's heirs and giving it to the grantee, thereby forcing the heir to take by descent if he takes at all. (The Rule originated in the case of <u>Wolfe v. Shelley</u>, K.B. 1581.) In the United States, the Rule has been abolished by statute in most jurisdictions. However, even in those states where it has been revoked, the Rule may still be applicable to instruments created before the Rule was repealed.

> If a freehold estate is given to a person and, in the same instrument, a remainder is given to the heirs (or the heirs of the body) of that person, that person takes both the freehold estate and the remainder.

The Rule applies only to remainders. A freehold estate is either a fee simple, a fee tail, or a life estate. Because a remainder cannot follow a fee simple, the estate prior to the remainder must be either a life estate or a fee tail. Since fee tails have been abolished almost everywhere in the U.S., in almost every case, the prior estate is a life estate. The Rule does not apply to executory interests. It operates only on remainders given to the heirs of the transferee. Shelley's Rule is a rule of law; its operation does not depend on the intent of the transferor or testator, but on whether or not the requirements of the Rule are satisfied.

Elements of the Rule in Shelley's Case

In order for the Rule to apply, the following four requirements must be satisfied:

i) one instrument,

ii) creating a freehold estate (almost always a life estate) in a transferee,

iii) creating a remainder in that transferee's heirs, and

iv) the interests must both be legal or both equitable.

If these requirements are met, the remainder is considered a remainder in fee simple in the transferee.

Ex: Radar ➔ Klinger for life, then to Klinger's heirs.

T	Radar to Klinger in <u>life estate</u>, then to Klinger's heirs in <u>fee simple</u>	
SoT	Klinger Klinger's heirs Radar	- life estate - contingent remainder in fee simple - reversion

The Rule in Shelley's Case applies. The interests should read:

M(SC)	Klinger Klinger	- life estate - vested remainder in fee simple

Initial parsing:

The words of purchase "to Klinger" denote Klinger as the grantee of the present possessory interest; thus, he receives the estate. The words of limitation "for life" identify the estate as a life estate.

The words of purchase "to Klinger's heirs" denote Klinger's heirs as the grantee(s) of a future interest. There are no words of limitation, so a fee simple is presumed. Klinger's heirs' interest is a remainder because (i) it is capable of becoming possessory immediately upon the expiration of the preceding estate and (ii) it cannot divest any other interests. It is a contingent remainder because, at the time of the conveyance, Klinger's heirs are unascertainable [you cannot point to them].

Radar retains a future interest known as a reversion. A reversion will always follow a contingent remainder because someone must hold seisin in the estate at all times. Since a contingent remainder is not certain to vest, the grantor must retain a reversion. If Klinger dies without heirs, then the estate would revert back to the grantor, Radar.

Application of the Rule in Shelley's Case:

There is (i) only one instrument creating a (ii) life estate in a transferee (Klinger), followed by (iii) a remainder in that transferee's (Klinger's) heirs, and (iv) both the life estate and remainder are legal interests.

Since the Rule in Shelley's Case applies, the conveyance is rewritten: "Radar ➔ Klinger for life, then to Klinger and heirs." The remainder in Klinger's heirs becomes a remainder in fee simple in Klinger. In effect, the Rule transmutes the words of purchase "Klinger's heirs" into words of limitation "Klinger and heirs."

Note: the third "box" in the above illustration is labeled "M (SC)". The "M" (for "marketability") indicates that we are applying one of the rules furthering marketability. The "SC" indicates that we are specifically applying the Rule in Shelley's Case.

Merger

The application of Shelley's Rule may trigger the Doctrine of Merger. Merger means that, whenever successive vested estates are owned by the same person, the two estates merge into a larger estate. Application of Shelley's Rule may create a situation in which the Doctrine of Merger can operate; but Shelley's Rule is entirely independent and distinct from the Doctrine of Merger. In the above example, the Doctrine of Merger could be applied, merging Klinger's life estate and vested remainder in fee simple. Klinger would be deemed to hold a fee simple absolute.

The Rule and Future Interests

The Rule in Shelley's Case can also apply to future interests.

Ex: Radar ➔ Klinger for life, then to Hawkeye for life, then to Hawkeye's heirs.

T	Radar to Klinger in <u>life estate</u>, then to Hawkeye in <u>life estate</u>, then to Hawkeye's heirs in <u>fee simple</u>	
SoT	Klinger	- life estate
	Hawkeye	- vested remainder in life estate
	Hawkeye's heirs	- contingent remainder in fee simple
	Radar	- reversion

The Rule in Shelley's Case applies. The interests should read:

M(SC)	Klinger	- life estate
	Hawkeye	- vested remainder in life estate
	Hawkeye	- vested remainder in fee simple

The Rule in Shelley's Case applies because there is one instrument creating a freehold estate in a transferee (Hawkeye), followed by a remainder in that transferee's (Hawkeye's) heirs (and both estates are legal.).

Note that after the application of the Rule in Shelley's Case, Klinger's life estate is left undisturbed. Shelley's Rule will only affect the part of the conveyance that grants a remainder in the transferee's heirs. The other portions of the conveyance will not be affected by the Rule.

The Doctrine of Merger may also apply in this case, merging Hawkeye's smaller life estate into his larger fee simple.

The Rule and Separated Interests

Shelley's Rule applies even though an intervening estate is interposed between the two interests.

Ex: Radar ➔ Klinger for life, then to Hawkeye for life, then to Klinger's heirs.

T	Radar to Klinger in life estate, then to Hawkeye in life estate, then to Klinger's heirs in fee simple	
SoT	Klinger Hawkeye Klinger's heirs Radar	- life estate - vested remainder in life estate - contingent remainder in fee simple - reversion

The Rule in Shelley's Case applies. The interests should read:

M(SC)	Klinger Hawkeye Klinger	- life estate - vested remainder in life estate - vested remainder in fee simple

We apply the Rule in Shelley's Case because there is one instrument creating a freehold estate in a transferee (Klinger) and followed by a remainder to the transferee's (Klinger's) heirs, and both the life estate and remainder are legal interests.

Note that Klinger's life estate and Hawkeye's intervening vested estate are left undisturbed. This is an instance where the Doctrine of Merger would not apply to merge Klinger's two interests (merger will not occur when a vested interest in a third party intervenes between the two interests).

Shelley's Rule Problems

In the following problems:

1. Read the conveyance.
2. Parse the state of title.
3. Ascertain if the Rule in Shelley's Case applies to the conveyance.
4. If it does, reform the state of title.

1.   Radar ➔ Hawkeye for life, then to Hawkeye's heirs.

T	
SoT	

M(SC)	

1.   Radar ➔ Hawkeye for life, then to Hawkeye's heirs.

T	Radar to Klinger in <u>life estate</u>, then to Hawkeye's heirs in <u>fee simple</u>	
SoT	Hawkeye Hawkeye's heirs Radar	- life estate - contingent remainder in fee simple - reversion

The Rule in Shelley's Case applies. The interests should read:

M(SC)	Klinger Hawkeye Hawkeye	- life estate - vested remainder in life estate - vested remainder in fee simple

Initial Parsing:

The words of purchase "to Hawkeye" denote Hawkeye as the grantee of the present possessory interest; thus, he receives the estate. The words of limitation "for life" identify the estate as a life estate.

The words of purchase "to Hawkeye's heirs" denote the grantee(s) of a future interest. There are no words of limitation, so a fee simple is presumed. The interest is a remainder because (i) it is capable of becoming possessory immediately upon the expiration of the preceding estate and (ii) it cannot divest any other interests. It is a contingent remainder because, at the time of the conveyance, Hawkeye's heirs are unascertainable.

Radar retains a future interest known as a reversion. A reversion will always follow a contingent remainder because someone must hold seisin in the estate at all times. Since a contingent remainder is not certain to vest, the grantor must retain a reversion.

Application of the Rule in Shelley's Case:

Shelley's Rule applies because there is one instrument creating life estate in a transferee, Hawkeye, followed by a remainder in that transferee's (Hawkeye's) heirs, and both the life estate and the remainder are legal interests. The remainder in Hawkeye's heirs becomes a remainder in fee simple in Hawkeye. In effect, the words of purchase ["Hawkeye's heirs"] become words of limitation ["Hawkeye and heirs"].

The Doctrine of Merger would apply in this situation, merging Hawkeye's life estate and vested remainder in fee simple into a fee simple absolute.

2.   Radar ➜ Klinger for life, then to Col. Potter for life, then to Klinger's heirs and their heirs.

T	
SoT	

M(SC)	

2. Radar ➔ Klinger for life, then to Col. Potter for life, then to Klinger's heirs and their heirs.

T	Radar to Klinger in <u>life estate</u>, then to Col. Potter in <u>life estate</u>, then to Klinger's heirs in <u>fee simple</u>	
SoT	Klinger Col. Potter Klinger's heirs Radar	- life estate - vested remainder in life estate - contingent remainder in fee simple - reversion

The Rule in Shelley's Case applies. The interests should read:

M(SC)	Klinger Col. Potter Klinger	- life estate - vested remainder in life estate - vested remainder in fee simple

Initial Parsing:

The words of purchase "to Klinger" denote Klinger as the grantee of the present possessory interest; thus, he receives the estate. The words of limitation "for life" identify the estate as a life estate.

The words of purchase "to Col. Potter" denote Col. Potter as the grantee of a future interest. The words of limitation "for life" identify the estate (that will exist if the future interest becomes possessory) as a life estate. The interest is a remainder because (i) it is capable of becoming possessory immediately upon the expiration of the preceding estate and (ii) it cannot divest any other interests. It is vested because Col. Potter is (i) ascertainable at the time of the conveyance and (ii) there is no condition precedent.

The words of purchase "to Klinger's heirs" denote the grantee(s) of a future interest. There are no words of limitation so a fee simple is presumed. The interest is a remainder because (i) it is capable of becoming possessory immediately upon the expiration of the preceding estate and (ii) it cannot divest any other interests. It is a contingent remainder because, at the time of the conveyance, Klinger's heirs are unascertainable.

Radar retains a future interest known as a reversion. A reversion will always follow a contingent remainder because someone must hold seisin in the estate at all times. Since a contingent remainder is not certain to vest, the grantor must retain a reversion.

Application of the Rule in Shelley's Case:

Shelley's Rule applies because there is one instrument creating a life estate in a transferee, Klinger, followed by a remainder in that transferee's (Klinger's) heirs, and both the life estate and the remainder are legal interests. The remainder in Klinger's heirs becomes a remainder in fee simple in Klinger. In effect, the words of purchase ["Klinger's heirs"] become words of limitation ["Klinger and heirs"].

The Doctrine of Merger would not apply in this case because it only applies when the two estates to be merged are successive and vested. Therefore, merger will not be affected where a vested estate in a third party intervenes between two estates.

3.   Col. Potter ➔ Radar for life, then to BJ for life, then to the heirs of Radar.

T	
SoT	

M(SC)	

3. Col. Potter ➜ Radar for life, then to BJ for life, then to the heirs of Radar.

T	Col. Potter to Radar in <u>life estate</u>, then to BJ in <u>life estate</u>, then to the heirs of Radar in <u>fee simple</u>	
SoT	Radar	- life estate
	BJ	- vested remainder in life estate
	Radar's heirs	- contingent remainder in fee simple
	Col. Potter	- reversion

The Rule in Shelley's Case applies. The interests should read:

M(SC)	Radar	- life estate
	BJ	- contingent remainder in life estate
	Radar	- vested remainder in fee simple

Initial Parsing:

The words of purchase "to Radar" denote Radar as the grantee of the present possessory interest; thus, he receives the estate. The words of limitation "for life" identify the estate as a life estate.

The words of purchase "to BJ" denote BJ as the grantee of a future interest. The words of limitation "for life" identify the estate (that will exist if the future interest becomes possessory) as a life estate. The interest is a remainder because (i) it is capable of becoming possessory immediately upon the expiration of the preceding estate and (ii) it cannot divest any other interests. It is a vested remainder because BJ is ascertainable [you can point to him] and (ii) it is not subject to a condition precedent.

The words of purchase "to Radar's heirs" denote the grantee(s) of a future interest. There are no words of limitation, so a fee simple is presumed. The interest is a remainder because it is capable of becoming possessory immediately upon the expiration of the preceding estate and it cannot divest any other interests. It is a contingent remainder because, at the time of the conveyance, Radar's heirs are unascertainable.

Col. Potter retains a future interest known as a reversion. A reversion will always follow a contingent remainder because someone must hold seisin in the estate at all times. Since a contingent remainder is not certain to vest, the grantor must retain a reversion.

Application of the Rule in Shelley's Case:

Shelley's Rule applies because there is one instrument creating a life estate in a transferee, Radar, followed by a remainder in that transferee's (Radar's) heirs, and both the life estate and the remainder are legal interests. The remainder in Radar's heirs becomes a remainder in fee simple in Radar. In effect, the words of purchase ["Radar's heirs"] become words of limitation ["Radar and heirs"].

The doctrine of merger will not apply since it is inapplicable to contingent interests.

4.   Radar ➔ Klinger for life, then to Frank Burns for life if he divorces his wife, then to Klinger's heirs.

T	
SoT	

M(SC)	

4. Radar ➜ Klinger for life, then to Frank Burns for life if he divorces his wife, then to Klinger's heirs.

T	Radar to Klinger in <u>life estate</u>, then to Frank Burns in <u>life estate</u> if he divorces his wife, then to Klinger's heirs in <u>fee simple</u>	
SoT	Klinger Frank Burns Klinger's heirs Radar	- life estate - contingent remainder in life estate - contingent remainder in fee simple - reversion

The Rule in Shelley's Case applies. The interests should read:

M(SC)	Klinger Frank Burns Klinger	- life estate - contingent remainder in life estate - vested remainder in fee simple

Initial Parsing:

The words of purchase "to Klinger" denote Klinger as the grantee of the present possessory interest; thus, he receives the estate. The words of limitation "for life" identify the estate as a life estate.

The words of purchase "to Frank Burns" denote Frank Burns as the grantee of a future interest. The words of limitation "for life" identify the estate (that will exist if the future interest becomes possessory) as a life estate. The interest is a remainder because (i) it is capable of becoming possessory immediately upon the expiration of the preceding estate and (ii) it cannot divest any other interests. It is a contingent remainder because it is subject to the condition precedent that Frank Burns divorce his wife.

The words of purchase "to Klinger's heirs" denote the grantee(s) of a future interest. There are no words of limitation, so a fee simple is presumed. The interest is a remainder because (i) it is capable of becoming possessory immediately upon the expiration of the preceding estate and (ii) it cannot divest any other interests. It is a contingent remainder because, at the time of the conveyance, Klinger's heirs are unascertainable.

Radar retains a future interest known as a reversion. A reversion will always follow a contingent remainder because someone must hold seisin in the estate at all times. Since a contingent remainder is not certain to vest, the grantor must retain a reversion.

Application of the Rule in Shelley's Case:

Shelley's Rule applies because there is one instrument creating a life estate in a transferee, Klinger, followed by a remainder in that transferee's (Klinger's) heirs, and both the life estate and the remainder are legal interests. The remainder in Klinger's heirs becomes a remainder in fee simple in Klinger. In effect, the words of purchase ["Klinger's heirs"] become words of limitation ["Klinger and heirs"]. The remainder in Klinger is vested since Klinger is ascertainable [you can point to him] and there is not condition precedent.

Note, in a jurisdiction that applies the Doctrine of Destructibility of Contingent Remainders, Frank Burn's intervening contingent remainder would be destroyed and Klinger's two vested interests would merge into a fee simple.

5.   Radar ➔ Charles for life, then to Radar's heirs.

T	
SoT	

M(SC)	

5.   Radar ➔ Charles for life, then to Radar's heirs.

T	Radar to Charles in <u>life estate</u>, then to Radar's heirs in <u>fee simple</u>	
SoT	Charles Radar's heirs Radar	- life estate - contingent remainder in fee simple - reversion

M(SC)	The Rule in Shelley's Case does not apply.

Initial Parsing:

The words of purchase "to Charles" denote Charles as the grantee of the present possessory interest; thus, he receives the estate. The words of limitation "for life" identify the estate as a life estate.

The words of purchase "to Radar's heirs" denote the grantee(s) of a future interest. There are no words of limitation, so a fee simple is presumed. The interest is a remainder because (i) it is capable of becoming possessory immediately upon the expiration of the preceding estate and (ii) it cannot divest any other interests. It is a contingent remainder because, at the time of the conveyance, Radar's heirs are not ascertainable.

Radar retains a future interest known as a reversion. A reversion will always follow a contingent remainder because someone must hold seisin in the estate at all times. Since a contingent remainder is not certain to vest, the grantor must retain a reversion.

Application of the Rule in Shelley's Case:

Shelley's Rule does not apply because the remainder is not in the transferee's (Charles') heirs; rather, it is in the transferor's (Radar's) heirs. [Note: the Doctrine of Worthier Title may apply.]

6.   Radar ➔ Charles for life, but if Klinger re-enlists, then to the heirs of Charles.

T	
SoT	

M(SC)	

6.   Radar ➔ Charles for life, but if Klinger re-enlists, then to the heirs of Charles.

T	Radar to Charles in <u>life estate</u>, but if Klinger re-enlists, then to the heirs of Charles in <u>fee simple</u>	
SoT	Charles	- life estate on executory limitation
	Charles's heirs	- shifting executory interest

M(SC)	The Rule in Shelley's Case does not apply.

Initial Parsing:

The words of purchase "to Charles" denote Charles as the grantee of the present possessory interest; thus, he receives the estate. The words of limitation "for life" identify the estate as a life estate. However, the words of limitation "but if" create a life estate defeasible. Since a defeasible estate is followed by a future interest in a third party, Charles has a life estate on executory limitation. His interest will be cut short if, and when, Klinger re-enlists.

The words of purchase "to the heirs of Charles" denote the grantee(s) of a future interest. There are no words of limitation, so a fee simple is presumed. Since Charles' heirs' future interest follows a defeasible estate, it is an executory interest. The interest of Charles' heirs will become possessory when Klinger re-enlists.

Application of the Rule in Shelley's Case:

Shelley's Rule does not apply because an executory interest, rather than a remainder, was created in the transferee's heirs. Shelley's Rule applies exclusively to remainders.

7.   Radar → Hawkeye for life, then to Honeycut for five years, then to the heirs of Hawkeye.

T	
SoT	

M(SC)	

7. Radar ➔ Hawkeye for life, then to Honeycut for five years, then to the heirs of Hawkeye.

T	Radar to Hawkeye in <u>life estate</u>, then to Honeycut for <u>a term of years</u>, then to the heirs of Hawkeye in <u>fee simple</u>	
SoT	Hawkeye	- life estate
	Honeycut	- vested remainder for a term of years
	Hawkeye's heirs	- contingent remainder in fee simple
	Radar	- reversion

The Rule in Shelley's Case applies. The interests should read:

M(SC)	Hawkeye	- life estate
	Honeycut	- vested remainder for a term of years
	Hawkeye	- vested remainder in fee simple

Initial Parsing:

The words of purchase "to Hawkeye" denote Hawkeye as the grantee of the present possessory interest; thus, he receives the estate. The words of limitation "for life" identify the estate as a life estate.

The words of purchase "to Honeycut" denote Honeycut as the grantee of a future interest. The words of limitation "for five years" identify the estate (that will exist if the future interest becomes possessory) as a term of years. Honeycut has a remainder because (i) it is capable of becoming possessory immediately upon the expiration of the preceding estate and (ii) it cannot divest the any other interests. It is a vested remainder because (i) Honeycut is ascertainable (you can point to him) and it is not subject to the condition precedent.

The words of purchase "to Hawkeye's heirs" denote the grantee(s) of a future interest. There are no words of limitation, so a fee simple is presumed. The interest is a remainder because (i) it is capable of becoming possessory immediately upon the expiration of the preceding estate and (ii) it cannot divest any other interests. It is a contingent remainder because, at the time of the conveyance, Hawkeye's heirs are unascertainable.

Radar retains a future interest known as a reversion. A reversion will always follow a contingent remainder because someone must hold seisin in the estate at all times. Since a contingent remainder is not certain to vest, the grantor must retain a reversion.

Application of the Rule in Shelley's Case:

Shelley's Rule applies because there is one instrument creating a life estate in a transferee, Hawkeye, followed by a remainder in that transferee's (Hawkeye's) heirs, and both the life estate and the remainder are legal interests. The remainder in Hawkeye's heirs becomes a remainder in fee simple in Hawkeye. In effect, the words of purchase ["Hawkeye's heirs"] become words of limitation ["Hawkeye and heirs"]. The remainder is vested because (i) Hawkeye is ascertainable [you can point to him] and (ii) there is no condition precedent.

Note, that in a jurisdiction that applies the Doctrine of Destructibility of Contingent Remainders (see DESTRUCTIBILITY), Honeycut's intervening contingent remainder would be destroyed and Hawkeye's two vested interests would merge into a fee simple.

8.   Radar ➔ Col. Potter as trustee for Klinger for life, then to Klinger's heirs.

T	
SoT	

M(SC)	

8.   Radar ➔ Col. Potter as trustee for Klinger for life, then to Klinger's heirs.

T	Radar to Col. Potter in trust in <u>fee simple</u> for Klinger in <u>life estate</u>, then to Klinger's heirs in <u>fee simple</u>	
SoT	Col. Potter	- legal fee simple
	Klinger	- equitable life estate
	Klinger's heirs	- equitable contingent remainder in fee simple
	Radar	- equitable reversion

The Rule in Shelley's Case applies: The interests should read:

M(SC)	Col. Potter	-legal fee simple
	Klinger	-equitable fee simple

Initial Parsing:

The words of purchase "to Col. Potter" denote Col. Potter as the grantee of the present legal interest. The words of limitation "as trustee" denote that Radar is creating a trust with Col. Potter as the trustee. Col. Potter holds legal title to the property as a trustee in fee simple. Klinger and Klinger's heirs hold the equitable interests of the trust. [A trust separates the responsibilities of ownership from the benefit of ownership. The individual who has the responsibilities of ownership and is responsible for the management of the assets is called the trustee and holds legal title. The individual who has the benefit of ownership and receives the income and/or principle disbursements is called the beneficiary and holds the equitable title.]

The words of purchase "for Klinger" denote Klinger as the grantee of an equitable present possessory interest; thus, he receives this estate. The words of limitation "for life" identify the estate as a life estate.

The words of purchase "to Klinger's heirs" denote the grantee(s) of a future interest. There are no words of limitation, so a fee simple is presumed. The interest is a remainder because (i) it is capable of becoming possessory immediately upon the expiration of the preceding estate and (ii) it cannot divest any other interests. It is a contingent remainder because, at the time of the conveyance, Klinger's heirs are unascertainable.

Radar retains a future interest known as a reversion. A reversion will always follow a contingent remainder because someone must hold seisin in the estate at all times. Since a contingent remainder is not certain to vest, the grantor must retain a reversion.

Application of the Rule in Shelley's Case:

Shelley's Rule applies because there is one instrument creating a life estate in a transferee, Klinger, followed by a remainder in that transferee's (Klinger's) heirs, and both the life estate and the remainder are equitable interests. The remainder in Klinger's heirs becomes a remainder in fee simple in Klinger. In effect, the words of purchase ["Klinger's heirs"] become words of limitation ["Klinger and heirs"].

The Doctrine of Merger would apply in this situation, merging Klinger's life estate and vested remainder into a fee simple absolute.

9.   First conveyance: Radar ➔ Klinger for life.

T	
SoT	

M(SC)	

Second conveyance: Radar ➔ Klinger's heirs, all my interest in Blackacre.

T	
SoT	

M(SC)	

9.   First conveyance: Radar ➔ Klinger for life.

T	Radar to Klinger in <u>life estate</u>
SoT	Klinger - life estate Radar - reversion

M(SC)	The Rule in Shelley's Case does not apply.

First conveyance:

The words of purchase "to Klinger" denote Klinger as the grantee of the present possessory interest; thus, he receives the estate. The words of limitation "for life" identify the estate as a life estate.

Radar retains a future interest known as a reversion. Radar's reversion will become possessory upon the expiration of Klinger's life estate.

Second conveyance: Radar ➔ Klinger's heirs, all my interest in Blackacre.

T	Radar to Klinger's heirs in <u>fee simple</u>
SoT	Klinger's heirs - reversion

M(SC)	The Rule in Shelley's Case does not apply.

Second conveyance:

The words of purchase "to Klinger's heirs" denote the grantee(s) of a future interest. There are no words of limitation, so a fee simple is presumed. Radar has conveyed his entire interest in the estate, which in this case is a reversion.

Application of the Rule in Shelley's Case:

Shelley's Rule would not apply in this instance because there are two instruments. The Rule requires that the interests in the transferee and the transferee's heirs must be created in the same instrument.

10.   Radar ➔ Klinger for life, then to Honeycut's heirs.

T	
SoT	

M(SC)	

10.   Radar ➜ Klinger for life, then to Honeycut's heirs.

T	Radar to Klinger in <u>life estate</u>, then to Honeycut's heirs in <u>fee simple</u>	
SoT	Klinger Honeycut's heirs Radar	- life estate - contingent remainder in fee simple - reversion

M(SC)	The Rule in Shelley's Case does not apply.

Initial Parsing:

The words of purchase "to Klinger" denote Klinger as the grantee of the present possessory interest; thus, he receives the estate. The words of limitation "for life" identify the estate as a life estate.

The words of purchase "to Honeycut's heirs" denote the grantee(s) of a future interest. There are no words of limitation, so a fee simple is presumed. The interest is a remainder because (i) it is capable of becoming possessory immediately upon the expiration of the preceding estate and (ii) it cannot divest any other interests. It is a contingent remainder because, at the time of the conveyance, Honeycut's heirs are unascertainable.

Radar retains a future interest known as a reversion. A reversion will always follow a contingent remainder because someone must hold seisin in the estate at all times. Since a contingent remainder is not certain to vest, the grantor must retain a reversion.

Application of the Rule in Shelley's Case:

Shelley's Rule would not apply in this instance because the remainder (in Honeycut's heirs) was not created in the life estate holder's (Klinger's) heirs.

Doctrine of Worthier Title

The Doctrine of Worthier Title was developed to further the marketability of land. At common law, the Doctrine of Worthier Title applied to any inter vivos conveyance of land in which a future interest was created in the grantor's own heirs. The rule provides that a grantor cannot create a remainder or executory interest in her own heirs. If the grantor attempts to create such an interest, that interest is void and the grantor is deemed to have retained a reversion. The Doctrine thus makes land more easily alienable by placing the future interest in the hands of an ascertainable grantor, rather than in the hands of her unascertainable heirs (remember that an individual does not have heirs until she dies).

> If a grantor creates a remainder or an executory interest in her own heirs, the grantor really retains a future interest in herself (a reversion) rather than creating a future interest in those heirs.

Thus, the Doctrine makes land more alienable by placing the interest with an identified individual (the grantor) rather than placing it with unascertained individuals who lack the capacity to transfer the interest.

Ex: Mr. Brady ➔ Alice for life, then to Mr. Brady's heirs.

T	Mr. Brady to Alice in <u>life estate</u>, then to Mr. Brady's heirs in <u>fee simple</u>	
SoT	Alice	- life estate
	Mr. Brady's heirs	- contingent remainder in fee simple
	Mr. Brady	- reversion

The Doctrine of Worthier Title applies. The interests should read:

M(SC)	Alice	- life estate
	Mr. Brady	- reversion

Since the remainder is a remainder in the grantor's heirs (Mr. Brady's heirs), the Doctrine of Worthier Title applies. The future interest in Mr. Brady's heirs becomes a future interest in Mr. Brady. In effect, the words of purchase ("to Mr. Brady's heirs") become words of limitation ("to Mr. Brady and heirs"). The contingent future interest in transferees becomes a vested future interest in the grantor (a reversion).

The Doctrine of Worthier Title does not apply to testamentary transfers in the United States.

Elements of the Doctrine of Worthier Title

The rule is applied when:

      i)   the conveyance creates a remainder or executory interest,

      ii)   in the GRANTOR's heirs

The remainder or executory interest becomes a future interest in the GRANTOR, rather than creating a future interest in the grantor's heirs. In effect, the contingent future interest in the heirs (they are unascertainable at the time of the grant) becomes a vested future interest in the grantor (who is ascertainable at the time of the grant).

Difference from the Rule in Shelley's Case

The Doctrine of Worthier Title is distinguishable from the Rule in Shelley's case. The Doctrine of Worthier Title applies to both remainders and executory interests created in the heirs of the grantor. The Rule in Shelley's Case is concerned only with remainders in the heirs of transferees.

Unlike the Rule in Shelley's Case, the preceding estate need not be any particular type. Commonly, the applicable future interest follows life estates, but it can also follow a term of years, a fee tail, or a defeasible fee simple.

Unlike the Rule in Shelley's Case, the interests are not required to be of the same type: one can be legal and the other equitable.

A Rule of Construction, Not a Rule of Law

The Doctrine of Worthier Title was initially a rule of law; but Judge Cardozo transformed the Doctrine into a rule of construction in the case of Doctor v. Hughes, 225 N.Y. 305, 122 N.E. 221 (1919). In the same decision, Judge Cardozo extended the Doctrine of Worthier Title to apply to personal property as well as real property. [This is an important extension because of its applicability to trusts.] As a rule of construction, the Doctrine of Worthier Title does not apply if the grantor clearly manifests an intent to create a future interest in his heirs; the doctrine applies only when it would operate to further the intent of the grantor. For a grantor to convey a valid remainder to his heirs, his intention to do so should be clearly expressed in the conveyance.

Doctrine of Worthier Title Problems

In the following problems:

1. Read the conveyance;
2. Initially parse the state of title;
3. Ascertain if the Doctrine of Worthier Title applies;
4. If it does, reform the state of title.

1.   Mr. Brady ➔ Marsha for life, then to Marsha's heirs.

       Fact: Mr. Brady is alive.

T	
SoT	

M(WT)	

1.   Mr. Brady ➔ Marsha for life, then to Marsha's heirs.

    Fact: Mr. Brady is alive.

T	Mr. Brady to Marsha in <u>life estate</u>, then to Marsha's heirs in <u>fee simple</u>	
SoT	Marsha	- life estate
	Marsha's heirs	- contingent remainder in fee simple
	Mr. Brady	- reversion

M(WT)	Doctrine of Worthier Title does not apply.

Initial Parsing:

The words of purchase "to Marsha" denote Marsha as the grantee of the present possessory interest; thus, she receives the estate. The words of limitation "for life" identify the estate as a life estate.

The words of purchase "to Marsha's heirs" denote the grantee(s) of a future interest. There are no words of limitation, so a fee simple is presumed. The interest is a remainder because (i)it is capable of becoming possessory immediately upon the expiration of the preceding estate and (ii)it cannot divest any prior interests. It is a contingent remainder because, at the time of the conveyance, Marsha's heirs are unascertainable.

Mr. Brady retains a future interest known as a reversion. A reversion will always follow a contingent remainder because someone must hold seisin in the estate at all times. Since a contingent remainder is not certain to vest, the grantor must retain a reversion.

Application of the Doctrine of Worthier Title:

The Doctrine of Worthier Title does not apply because the remainder is to Marsha's heirs, and not to the grantor's (Mr. Brady's) heirs. [Note: Shelley's Rule may apply.]

2.   Mr. Brady ➜ Marsha for life, then to Mr. Brady's heirs.

Fact: Mr. Brady is alive.

T	
SoT	

M(WT)	

2. Mr. Brady ➔ Marsha for life, then to Mr. Brady's heirs.

Fact: Mr. Brady is alive.

T	Mr. Brady to Marsha in <u>life estate</u>, then to Mr. Brady's heirs in <u>fee simple</u>	
SoT	Marsha Mr. Brady's heirs Mr. Brady	- life estate - contingent remainder in fee simple - reversion

Doctrine of Worthier Title applies. The interests should read:

M(WT)	Marsha Mr. Brady	- life estate - reversion

Initial Parsing:

The words of purchase "to Marsha" denote Marsha as the grantee of the present possessory interest; thus, she receives the estate. The words of limitation "for life" identify the estate as a life estate.

The words of purchase "to Mr. Brady's heirs" denote the grantee(s) of a future interest. There are no words of limitation, so a fee simple is presumed. The interest is a remainder because (i) it is capable of becoming possessory immediately upon the expiration of the preceding estate and (ii) it cannot divest any other interests. It is a contingent remainder because, at the time of the conveyance, Mr. Brady's heirs are unascertainable.

Mr. Brady retains a future interest known as a reversion. A reversion will always follow a contingent remainder because someone must hold seisin in the estate at all times. Since a contingent remainder is not certain to vest, the grantor must retain a reversion.

Application of the Doctrine of Worthier Title:

The Doctrine of Worthier Title applies because the conveyance is inter vivos, and a remainder was created in the grantor's heirs. Under the rule, the presumption is that no interest is created in Mr. Brady's heirs; rather Mr. Brady (the grantor) intends to retain a reversion. In effect, the words of purchase ("to Mr. Brady's heirs") become words of limitation ("to Mr. Brady and heirs").

3.   Mr. Brady ➔ Marsha for life, then to Jan for life, then to Marsha's heirs.

       Fact: Mr. Brady is alive.

T	
SoT	

M(WT)	

3. Mr. Brady ➔ Marsha for life, then to Jan for life, then to Marsha's heirs.

Fact: Mr. Brady is alive.

T	Mr. Brady to Marsha in <u>life estate</u>, then to Jan in <u>life estate</u>, then to Marsha's heirs in <u>fee simple</u>	
SoT	Marsha	- life estate
	Jan	- vested remainder in life estate
	Marsha's heirs	- contingent remainder in fee simple
	Mr. Brady	- reversion

M(WT)	Doctrine of Worthier Title does not apply.

Initial Parsing:

The words of purchase "to Marsha" denote Marsha as the grantee of the present possessory interest; thus, she receives the estate. The words of limitation "for life" identify the estate as a life estate.

The words of purchase "to Jan" denote Jan as the grantee of a future interest. The words of limitation "for life" identify the estate (that will exist if the future interest becomes possessory) as a life estate. The interest is a remainder because (i) it is capable of becoming possessory immediately upon the expiration of the preceding estate and (ii) it cannot divest any other interests. It is vested because Jan is (i) ascertainable at the time of the conveyance and (ii) there is no condition precedent.

The words of purchase "to Marsha's heirs" denote the grantee(s) of a future interest. There are no words of limitation, so a fee simple is presumed. The interest is a remainder because (i) it is capable of becoming possessory immediately upon the expiration of the preceding estate and (ii) it cannot divest any other interests. It is a contingent remainder because, at the time of the conveyance, Marsha's heirs are unascertainable.

Mr. Brady retains a future interest known as a reversion. A reversion will always follow a contingent remainder because someone must hold seisin in the estate at all times. Since a contingent remainder is not certain to vest, the grantor must retain a reversion.

Application of the Doctrine of Worthier Title:

The Doctrine of Worthier Title does not apply because the remainder is to Marsha's heir and not to the grantor's (Mr. Brady's) heirs. [Note: Shelley's Rule may apply.]

4.   Mr. Brady ➔ Peter for life, then to Bobby's heirs.

Facts: Mr. Brady and Bobby are alive.

T	
SoT	

M(WT)	

4. Mr. Brady ➔ Peter for life, then to Bobby's heirs.

    Facts: Mr. Brady and Bobby are alive.

T	Mr. Brady to Peter in <u>life estate</u>, then to Bobby's heirs in <u>fee simple</u>	
SoT	Peter Bobby's heirs Mr. Brady	- life estate - contingent remainder in fee simple - reversion

M(WT)	Doctrine of Worthier Title does not apply.

Initial Parsing:

The words of purchase "to Peter" denote Peter as the grantee of the present possessory interest; thus, he receives the estate. The words of limitation "for life" identify the estate as a life estate.

The words of purchase "to Bobby's heirs" denote the grantee(s) of a future interest. There are no words of limitation, so a fee simple is presumed. The interest is a remainder because (i) it is capable of becoming possessory immediately upon the expiration of the preceding estate and (ii) it cannot divest any other interests. It is a contingent remainder because, at the time of the conveyance, Bobby's heirs are unascertainable.

Mr. Brady retains a future interest known as a reversion. A reversion will always follow a contingent remainder because someone must hold seisin in the estate at all times. Since a contingent remainder is not certain to vest, the grantor must retain a reversion.

Application of the Doctrine of Worthier Title:

The Doctrine of Worthier Title does not apply because the remainder is in Bobby's heirs and not in the grantor's (Mr. Brady's) heirs. [Note: Shelley's Rule does not apply either because there is no remainder in the life estate holder's heirs.]

5. Mr. Brady ➜ Mrs. Brady for life, then to Alice and the heirs of her body, then to Mr.
                 Brady's heirs.

    Facts: This grant is by will and Mr. Brady is dead.

T	
SoT	

M(WT)	

5.   Mr. Brady ➔   Mrs. Brady for life, then to Alice and the heirs of her body, then to Mr. Brady's heirs.

Fact: This grant is by will and Mr. Brady is dead.

T	Mr. Brady to Mrs. Brady in <u>life estate</u>, then to Alice in <u>fee tail</u>, then to Mr. Brady's heirs in <u>fee simple</u>	
SoT	Mrs. Brady	- life estate
	Alice	- vested remainder in fee tail
	Mr. Brady's heirs	- vested remainder in fee simple

M(WT)	Doctrine of Worthier Title does not apply.

Initial parsing:

The words of purchase "to Mrs. Brady" denote Mrs. Brady as the grantee of the present possessory interest; thus, she receives the estate. The words of limitation "for life" identify the estate as a life estate.

The words of purchase "to Alice" denote Alice as the grantee of a future interest. The words of limitation "and the heirs of her body" identify the estate (that will exist if the future interest becomes possessory) as a fee tail. The interest is a remainder because (i) it is capable of becoming possessory immediately upon the expiration of the preceding estate and (ii) it cannot divest any other interests. It is vested because (i) Alice is ascertainable at the time of the conveyance and (ii) there is no condition precedent.

The words of purchase "to Mr. Brady's heirs" denote the grantee(s) of a future interest. There are no words of limitation, so a fee simple is presumed. The interest is a remainder because (i) it is capable of becoming possessory immediately upon the expiration of the preceding estate and (ii) it cannot divest any other interests. It is vested because (i) Mr. Brady's heirs are ascertainable [Mr. Brady is dead] and (ii) there is no condition precedent.

Application of the Doctrine of Worthier Title:

The Doctrine of Worthier Title does not apply because this is a testamentary transfer, not an inter vivos conveyance. [The Doctrine of Worthier Title was promulgated to further marketability. A conveyance to individuals who were unascertainable at the time of the grant left property unmarketable. However, a will that contains a transfer to the grantor's heirs does not present a marketability problem because the grantor's heirs are ascertainable at the time of the grantor's death (the moment when the will is operative).]

6.   Mr. Brady ➔   Mrs. Brady for life, then to Alice and the heirs of her body, then to Mr. Brady's heirs.

Fact: Mr. Brady is alive.

T	
SoT	

M(WT)	

6.　　　Mr. Brady ➜　Mrs. Brady for life, then to Alice and the heirs of her body, then to Mr. Brady's heirs.

Fact:　Mr. Brady is alive.

T	Mr. Brady to Mrs. Brady in <u>life estate</u>, then to Alice in <u>fee tail</u>, then to Mr. Brady's heirs in <u>fee simple</u>	
SoT	Mrs. Brady	- life estate
	Alice	- vested remainder in fee tail
	Mr. Brady's heirs	- contingent remainder in fee simple
	Mr. Brady	- reversion

Doctrine of Worthier Title applies.　The interest should read:

M(WT)	Mrs. Brady	- life estate
	Alice	- vested remainder in fee tail
	Mr. Brady	- reversion

Initial Parsing:

The words of purchase "to Mrs. Brady" denote Mrs. Brady as the grantee of the present possessory interest; thus, she receives the estate.　The words of limitation "for life" identify the estate as a life estate.

The words of purchase "to Alice" denote Alice as the grantee of a future interest.　The words of limitation "and the heirs of her body" identify the estate (that will exist if the future interest becomes possessory) as a fee tail.　Alice's interest is a remainder because (i) it is capable of becoming possessory immediately upon the expiration of the preceding estate and (ii) it cannot divest any other interests.　It is vested because (i) Alice is ascertainable at the time of the conveyance and (ii) there is no condition precedent.

The words of purchase "to Mr. Brady's heirs" denote the grantees of a future interest.　There are no words of limitation, a fee simple is presumed.　The interest is a remainder because (i) it is capable of becoming possessory immediately upon the expiration of the preceding estate and (ii) it cannot divest any other interests.　It is a contingent remainder because, at the time of the conveyance, Mr. Brady's heirs are unascertainable.

Mr. Brady has a future interest known as a reversion.　A reversion will always follow a contingent remainder because someone must hold seisin in the estate at all times.　Since a contingent remainder is not certain to vest, the grantor must retain a reversion.

Application of the Doctrine of Worthier Title:

The Doctrine of Worthier Title applies because the conveyance is inter vivos and a remainder was created in the grantor's heirs.　Under the rule, the presumption is that no interest is created in Mr. Brady's heirs; rather Mr. Brady (the grantor) intends to retain a future interest in himself.　In effect, the words of purchase ("to Mr. Brady's heirs") become words of limitation ("to Mr. Brady and heirs").

7. Mr. Brady ➜ Alice for life, then if Jan gets married, to Cindy for life, then to Mr. Brady's heirs.

    Fact: Mr. Brady is alive.

T	
SoT	

M(WT)	

7.   Mr. Brady ➔   Alice for life, then if Jan gets married, to Cindy for life, then to Mr. Brady's heirs.

Fact: Mr. Brady is alive.

T	Mr. Brady to Alice in <u>life estate</u>, then if Jan gets married, to Cindy in <u>life estate</u>, then to Mr. Brady's heirs in <u>fee simple</u>	
SoT	Alice	- life estate
	Cindy	- contingent remainder in life estate
	Mr. Brady's heirs	- contingent remainder in fee simple
	Mr. Brady	- reversion

Doctrine of Worthier Title applies. The interests should read:

M(WT)	Alice	- life estate
	Cindy	- contingent remainder in life estate
	Mr. Brady	- reversion

Initial Parsing:

The words of purchase "to Alice" denote Alice as the grantee of the present possessory interest; thus, she receives the estate. The words of limitation "for life" identify the estate as a life estate.

The words of purchase "to Cindy" denote Cindy as the grantee of a future interest. The words of limitation "for life" identify the estate (that will exist if the future interest becomes possessory) as a life estate. Cindy's interest is a remainder because (i) it is capable of becoming possessory immediately upon the expiration of the preceding estate and (ii) it cannot divest any other interests. It is a contingent remainder because it is subject to the condition precedent that Jan marries.

The words of purchase "to Mr. Brady's heirs" denote the grantee(s) of a future interest. There are no words of limitation, so a fee simple is presumed. The interest is a remainder because (i) it is capable of becoming possessory immediately upon the expiration of the preceding estate and (ii) it cannot divest any other interests. It is a contingent remainder because, at the time of the conveyance, Mr. Brady's heirs are unascertainable.

Mr. Brady has a future interest known as a reversion. A reversion will always follow a contingent remainder because someone must hold seisin in the estate at all times. Since a contingent remainder is not certain to vest, the grantor must retain a reversion.

Application of the Doctrine of Worthier Title:

The Doctrine of Worthier Title applies because the conveyance is inter vivos and a remainder was created in the grantor's heirs. Under the rule, the presumption is that no interest is created in Mr. Brady's heirs; rather Mr. Brady (the grantor) intends to retain a future interest in himself. In effect, the words of purchase ("to Mr. Brady's heirs") become words of limitation ("to Mr. Brady and heirs").

8.　　　Mr. Brady ➔　Marsha for life, then to Cindy for life if she becomes a lawyer, then to Peter for life if he becomes a doctor, then to Mr. Brady's heirs.

Fact:　Mr. Brady is alive.

T	
SoT	

M(WT)	

8. Mr. Brady ➔ Marsha for life, then to Cindy for life if she becomes a lawyer, then to Peter for life if he becomes a doctor, then to Mr. Brady's heirs.

Fact: Mr. Brady is alive.

T	Mr. Brady to Marsha in <u>life estate</u>, then to Cindy in <u>life estate</u> if she becomes a lawyer, then to Peter in <u>life estate</u> if he becomes a doctor, then to Mr. Brady's heirs in <u>fee simple</u>	
SoT	Marsha	- life estate
	Cindy	- contingent remainder in life estate
	Peter	- contingent remainder in life estate
	Mr. Brady's heirs	- contingent remainder in fee simple
	Mr. Brady	- reversion

The Doctrine of Worthier Title applies. The interests should read:

M(WT)	Marsha	- life estate
	Cindy	- contingent remainder in life estate
	Peter	- contingent remainder in life estate
	Mr. Brady	- reversion

Initial Parsing:

The words of purchase "to Marsha" denote Marsha as the grantee of the present possessory interest; thus, she receives the estate. The words of limitation "for life" identify the estate as a life estate.

The words of purchase "to Cindy" denote Cindy as the grantee of a future interest. The words of limitation "for life" identify the estate (that will exist if the future interest becomes possessory) as a life estate. The interest is a remainder because (i) it is capable of becoming possessory immediately upon the expiration of the preceding estate and (ii) it cannot divest any other interests. It is a contingent remainder because it is subject to the condition precedent that Cindy become a lawyer. Note that this is not an alternative contingent remainder as both Cindy's and Peter's interests may vest.

The words of purchase "to Peter" denote Peter as the grantee of a future interest. The words of limitation "for life" identify the estate (that will exist if the future interest becomes possessory) as a life estate. The interest is a remainder because (i) it is capable of becoming possessory immediately upon the expiration of the preceding estate and (ii) it cannot divest any other interests. It is a contingent remainder because it is subject to the condition precedent that Peter become a doctor. Note that this is not an alternative contingent remainder as both Cindy's and Peter's interests may vest.

The words of purchase "to Mr. Brady's heirs" denote the grantee(s) of a future interest. There are no words of limitation, so a fee simple is presumed. The interest is a remainder because (i) it is capable of becoming possessory immediately upon the expiration of the preceding estate and (ii) it cannot divest any other interests. It is a contingent remainder because, at the time of the conveyance, Mr. Brady's heirs are unascertainable.

Mr. Brady retains a future interest known as a reversion. A reversion will always follow a contingent remainder because someone must hold seisin in the estate at all times. Since a contingent remainder is not certain to vest, the grantor must retain a reversion.

Application of the Doctrine of Worthier Title:

The Doctrine of Worthier Title applies because the conveyance is inter vivos and a remainder was created in the grantor's heirs. Under the rule, the presumption is that no interest is created in Mr. Brady's heirs; rather Mr. Brady (the grantor) intends to retain a future interest in himself. In effect, the words of purchase "(to Mr. Brady's heirs") become words of limitation ("to Mr. Brady and heirs").

9.   Mr. Brady ➔   Alice for life, then to Sam the Butcher for life, then to Mr. Brady's children.

Facts: Mr. Brady is alive and has two children, Greg and Peter.

T	
SoT	

M(WT)	

9.   Mr. Brady ➔   Alice for life, then to Sam the Butcher for life, then to Mr. Brady's children.

Facts: Mr. Brady is alive and has two children, Greg and Peter.

T	Mr. Brady to Alice in <u>life estate</u>, then to Sam the Butcher in <u>life estate</u>, then to Mr. Brady's children in <u>fee simple</u>	
SoT	Alice	- life estate
	Sam the Butcher	- vested remainder in life estate
	Mr. Brady's children	- vested remainder in fee simple subject to open

M(WT)	Doctrine of Worthier Title does not apply.

Initial Parsing:

The words of purchase "to Alice" denote Alice as the grantee of the present possessory interest; thus, she receives the estate. The words of limitation "for life" identify the estate as a life estate.

The words of purchase "to Sam the Butcher" denote Sam as the grantee of a future interest. The words of limitation "for life" identify the estate (that will exist if the future interest becomes possessory) as a life estate. The interest is a remainder because (i) it is capable of becoming possessory immediately upon the expiration of the preceding estate and (ii) it cannot divest any other interests. It is vested because (i) Sam is ascertainable at the time of the conveyance and (ii) there is no condition precedent.

The words of purchase "to Mr. Brady's children" denote them as the grantees of a future interest. There are no words of limitation, so a fee simple is presumed. The interest is a remainder because (i) it is capable of becoming possessory immediately upon the expiration of the preceding estate and (ii) it cannot divest any other interests. It is vested because (i) Greg and Peter are ascertainable at the time of the conveyance and (ii) there is no condition precedent. However, the vested remainder is subject to open because Mr. Brady may have more children, so the class is not yet closed.

Application of the Doctrine of Worthier Title:

The Doctrine of Worthier Title does not apply because the remainder is to the grantor's (Mr. Brady's) children and not to the grantor's (Mr. Brady's) heirs. Even though Mr. Brady's children may be heirs one day (and therefore are currently heirs apparent), for the Doctrine to apply, the conveyance must read "to Mr. Brady's heirs."

10.   Mr. Brady ➔   Greg for life, then to Bobby provided that it is used as a school, but if it is
no longer used as a school, then to Mr. Brady's heirs.

Fact: Mr. Brady is alive.

T	
SoT	

M(WT)	

10.   Mr. Brady ➜   Greg for life, then to Bobby provided that it is used as a school, but if it is
no longer used as a school, then to Mr. Brady's heirs.

Fact: Mr. Brady is alive.

T	Mr. Brady to Greg in <u>life estate</u>, then to Bobby in <u>fee simple</u> **provided that** it is used as a school, but if it is no longer used as a school, then to Mr. Brady's heirs in <u>fee simple</u>	
SoT	Greg	- life estate
	Bobby	- vested remainder in fee simple on executory limitation
	Mr. Brady's heirs	- shifting executory interest in fee simple

The Doctrine of Worthier Title applies. The interests should read:

M(WT)	Greg	- life estate
	Bobby	- vested remainder in fee simple subject to a condition subsequent
	Mr. Brady	- right of entry

Initial Parsing:

The words of purchase "to Greg" denote Greg as the grantee of the present possessory interest; thus, he receives the estate. The words of limitation "for life" identify the estate as a life estate.

The words of purchase "to Bobby" denote Bobby as the grantee of a future interest. There are no words of limitation, so a fee simple is presumed. However, the words of limitation "provided that" create a defeasible fee. Since the defeasible fee is followed by a future interest in a third party, Bobby has a fee simple on executory limitation. The interest is a remainder because (i) it is capable of becoming possessory immediately upon the expiration of the preceding estate and (ii) it cannot divest any other interests. It is vested because (i) Bobby is ascertainable at the time of the conveyance and (ii) there is no condition precedent. His interest will be cut short if the property fails to be used as a school.

The words of purchase "to Mr. Brady's heirs" denote the grantee(s) of a future interest. There are no words of limitation, so a fee simple is presumed. Since Mr. Brady's heirs' future interest follows a defeasible fee, it is an executory interest. It is a shifting interest because Mr. Brady's heirs, transferees, will divest Bobby, another transferee, of the estate. The interest of Mr. Brady's heirs will become possessory if the property fails to be used as a school.

Application of the Doctrine of Worthier Title:

The Doctrine of Worthier Title applies because the conveyance is inter vivos and an executory interest was created in the grantor's heirs. Under the rule, the presumption is that no interest is created in Mr. Brady's heirs; rather Mr. Brady intends to retain a future interest in himself. In short, the words of purchase (to Mr. Brady's heirs) become words of limitation (to Mr. Brady and heirs). Because this future interest in the grantor follows a fee simple subject to condition subsequent (again, after the application of the Doctrine of Worthier Title, there is no "flow" to a third party and therefore the fee simple on executory limitation becomes a fee simple subject to condition subsequent), it is referred to as a right of entry.

Destructibility of Contingent Remainders

In a destructibility jurisdiction, a contingent remainder is destroyed if it does not vest at, or before, the termination of the previous freehold estate. If the holder of the remainder cannot take seisin at the expiration of the preceding estate, then that contingent remainder is lost, and seisin moves on to the next vested estate. In other words, if at the expiration of the preceding estate (i) a condition precedent is not fulfilled or (ii) the holder of the remainder continues to be unascertained, then the remainder is destroyed.

Ex: Jack ➜ Chrissy for life, then to Janet and her heirs if Janet marries.

T	Jack to Chrissy in <u>life estate</u>, then to Janet in <u>fee simple</u> if Janet marries	
SoT	Chrissy Janet Jack	- life estate - contingent remainder in fee simple - reversion

The words of purchase "to Chrissy" denote Chrissy as the grantee of the present possessory interest; thus, she receives the estate. The words of limitation "for life" identify the estate as a life estate.

The words of purchase "to Janet" denote Janet as the grantee of a future interest. The words of limitation "and her heirs" identify the estate as a fee simple. The interest is a remainder because it is capable of becoming possessory immediately upon the expiration of the preceding estate and it cannot divest any other interests. It is contingent because it is subject to the condition precedent that Janet get married.

Jack retains a future interest known as a reversion which is a future interest in the grantor. A reversion will always follow a contingent remainder because someone must hold seisin in the estate at all times. Since a contingent remainder is not certain to vest, the grantor must retain a reversion.

As the title of this doctrine suggests, only contingent remainders are destroyed. The doctrine of destructibility is not applied to executory interests.

Destructibility Jurisdiction

If Janet is not married by the time of Chrissy's death, i.e., if the condition precedent is not fulfilled by the end of the preceding interest, Janet's contingent remainder is "destroyed," and she loses any and all interest. Jack's reversion then becomes possessory. Giving seisin back to Jack promotes marketability, as Jack can re-grant the land to someone else. If Jack still wants Janet to have the land, Jack must reconvey the land to Janet.

Non-Destructibility Jurisdiction

The general rule in a non-destructibility jurisdiction is that if the holder of the remainder is not ready to take seisin upon the expiration of the preceding estate, then seisin reverts back to the grantor until the holder is ready to take possession. When his reversion becomes possessory, Jack has a fee simple on executory limitation -- that is capable of being divested by Janet if Janet fulfills the condition precedent. The contingent remainder becomes an executory interest (because it will divest the grantor of the fee). It is a springing interest because Janet, a transferee, will divest Jack, the transferor, of the estate.

Thus, in the above example, if Janet is not married at the time of Chrissy's death, then Jack's reversion becomes possessory (Jack holds a fee simple on executory limitation), and Janet's remainder becomes a springing executory interest. Jack holds possession until Janet gets married or until the condition is no longer capable of being performed (Janet's death). Upon Janet's marriage, Janet's interest becomes possessory, and Jack gives up possession.

Destructibility of Contingent Remainders
Problems

1. Jack ➔ Janet for life, then to Chrissy if she becomes a lawyer.

T	
SoT	

1.   Jack ➜ Janet for life, then to Chrissy if she becomes a lawyer.

T	Jack to Janet in <u>life estate</u>, then to Chrissy in <u>fee simple</u> if she becomes a lawyer	
SoT	Janet	- life estate
	Chrissy	- contingent remainder in fee simple
	Jack	- reversion

The words of purchase "to Janet" denote Janet as the grantee of the present possessory interest; thus, she receives the estate. The words of limitation "for life" identify the estate as a life estate.

The words of purchase "to Chrissy" denote Chrissy as the grantee of a future interest. There are no words of limitation, so a fee simple is presumed. The interest is a remainder because (i)it is capable of becoming possessory immediately upon the expiration of the preceding estate and (ii) it cannot divest any other interests. It is a contingent remainder because it is subject to the condition precedent that Chrissy become a lawyer.

Jack retains a future interest known as a reversion. A reversion will always follow a contingent remainder because someone must hold seisin in the estate at all times. Since a contingent remainder is not certain to vest, the grantor must retain a reversion.

DESTRUCTIBILITY JURISDICTION: If Chrissy does not become a lawyer by the time Janet dies, Chrissy's contingent remainder is "destroyed," and she loses any and all interest. Jack's reversion would then become possessory.

NON-DESTRUCTIBILITY JURISDICTION: If Chrissy does not become a lawyer by the time Janet dies, then the estate would revert to the grantor, Jack, to hold in fee simple on executory limitation until the condition is satisfied or until it is no longer capable of being performed (Chrissy's death). At this point, Chrissy's interest becomes a springing executory interest. It is an executory interest because it follows a fee simple on executory limitation; it is springing because Chrissy, a transferee, would divest Jack, the transferor.

2. Mr. Roper ➔ Jack for ever and ever, but if he ever marries Larry, then to Chrissy.

T	
SoT	

2.   Mr. Roper ➜ Jack for ever and ever, but if he ever marries Larry, then to Chrissy.

T	Mr. Roper to Jack in <u>fee simple</u>, but if he ever marries Larry, then to Chrissy in <u>fee simple</u>	
SoT	Jack Chrissy	- fee simple on executory limitation - shifting executory interest

The words of purchase "to Jack" denote Jack as the grantee of the present possessory interest; thus, he receives the estate. "For ever and ever" are not words of limitation, but they reflect Mr. Roper's intent to give his entire interest, so the interest is construed modernly as a fee simple. However, the words of limitation "but if" create a fee simple subject to condition subsequent, which is a defeasible fee. Since a third party, Chrissy, will divest Jack of his estate, Jack has a fee simple on executory limitation. Jack will lose the estate if he ever marries Larry.

The words of purchase "to Chrissy" denote Chrissy as the grantee of a future interest. There are no words of limitation, so a fee simple is presumed. Chrissy's interest is an executory interest because a remainder cannot follow a fee simple. It is a shifting interest because Chrissy, a transferee, will divest Jack, another transferee, of the estate.

Jack receives a fee simple on executory limitation to do with as he pleases. He will only be divested of the estate if he marries Larry. If Jack marries Larry, Chrissy's interest will vest. If Jack never marries Larry, Chrissy's interest will never vest.

DESTRUCTIBILITY JURISDICTION: Destructibility is not applicable to this conveyance because no contingent remainders were created. The conveyance will be treated the same in both destructibility and non-destructibility jurisdictions.

3.   Janet ➔ Chrissy for life, then to Jack if he marries Vicki.

T	
SoT	

3.   Janet ➜ Chrissy for life, then to Jack if he marries Vicki.

T	Janet to Chrissy in <u>life estate</u>, then to Jack in <u>fee simple</u> if he marries Vicki
SoT	Chrissy - life estate Jack - contingent remainder in fee simple Janet - reversion

The words of purchase "to Chrissy" denote Chrissy as the grantee of the present possessory interest; thus, she receives the estate. The words of limitation "for life" identify the estate as a life estate.

The words of purchase "to Jack" denote Jack as the grantee of a future interest. There are no words of limitation, so a fee simple is presumed. Jack's interest is a remainder because (i) it is capable of becoming possessory immediately upon the expiration of the preceding estate and (ii) it cannot divest any other interests. It is a contingent remainder because it is subject to the condition precedent that Jack marry Vicki before he can take possession of the estate.

Janet retains a future interest known as a reversion. A reversion will always follow a contingent remainder because someone must hold seisin in the estate at all times. Since contingent remainders are not certain to vest, the grantor must retain a reversion.

DESTRUCTIBILITY JURISDICTION: If Jack is not married when Chrissy dies, his contingent remainder would be "destroyed," and he loses any and all interest in the estate. Janet's reversion would then become possessory.

NON-DESTRUCTIBILITY JURISDICTION: If Jack is not married when Chrissy dies, then the estate would revert to the grantor, Janet, to hold in fee simple on executory limitation until the condition is satisfied or until the condition is no longer capable of being performed (Jack's death). At this point, Jack's interest becomes a springing executory interest. It is an executory interest because it follows a fee simple on executory limitation; it is springing because Jack, a transferee, would divest Janet, the transferor.

4.   Mrs. Roper ➔ Jack for life, then to Jack's children.

          Fact: Jack has a son, Chuckie.

T	
SoT	

4.   Mrs. Roper ➜ Jack for life, then to Jack's children.

        Fact: Jack has a son, Chuckie.

T	Mrs. Roper to Jack in <u>life estate</u>, then to Jack's children in <u>fee simple</u>	
SoT	Jack	- life estate
	Jack's children	- vested remainder in fee simple subject to open

The words of purchase "to Jack" denote Jack as the grantee of the present possessory interest; thus, he receives the estate. The words of limitation "for life" identify the estate as a life estate.

The words of purchase "to Jack's children" denote them as the grantee(s) of a future interest. There are no words of limitation, so a fee simple is presumed. The interest is a remainder because (i) it is capable of becoming possessory immediately upon the expiration of the preceding estate and (ii) it cannot divest any other interests. It is vested because, at the time of the conveyance (i) Jack's son, Chuckie, is ascertainable [you can point to him] and (ii) there is no condition precedent. It is subject to open because after the conveyance Jack could have additional children who would also have an interest in the estate.

DESTRUCTIBILITY JURISDICTION: Destructibility does not apply because there is no contingent remainder.

5. Chrissy ➔ Jack as long as Sacramento remains the capitol of California.

T	
SoT	

5.   Chrissy ➔ Jack as long as Sacramento remains the capitol of California.

T	Chrissy to Jack in <u>fee simple</u> **as long as** Sacramento remains the capitol of California
SoT	Jack - fee simple determinable Chrissy - possibility of reverter

The words of purchase "to Jack" denote Jack as the grantee of the present possessory interest; thus, he receives the estate. There are no words of limitation, so a fee simple is presumed. However, the words of limitation "as long as" create a fee simple determinable, which is a defeasible fee. Jack will hold the estate for as long as Sacramento remains the capitol of California.

Chrissy, the grantor, retains a future interest known as a possibility of reverter. The interest becomes possessory automatically upon the happening of the stated event. Chrissy's future interest will become possessory if, and when, Sacramento ceases to be the capitol of California.

DESTRUCTIBILITY JURISDICTION: Destructibility does not apply because there is no contingent remainder.

6.   Jack ➔ Larry for life, then to Larry's first born son.

Fact: Larry has no children.

T	
SoT	

6.   Jack ➜ Larry for life, then to Larry's first born son.

Fact: Larry has no children.

T	Jack to Larry in <u>life estate</u>, then to Larry's first born son in <u>fee simple</u>
SoT	Larry — life estate First Born Son — contingent remainder fee simple Jack — reversion

The words of purchase "to Larry" denote Larry as the grantee of the present possessory interest; thus, he receives the estate. The words of limitation "for life" identify the estate as a life estate.

The words of purchase "to Larry's first born son" denote Larry's first born son as the grantee of a future interest. There are no words of limitation, so a fee simple is presumed. The interest is a remainder because (i) it is capable of becoming possessory immediately upon the expiration of the preceding estate and (ii) it cannot divest any other interests. It is contingent because, at the time of the conveyance, Larry's first born son is unascertainable.

Jack retains a future interest known as a reversion. A reversion will always follow a contingent remainder because someone must hold seisin in the estate at all times. Since contingent remainders are not certain to vest, the grantor must retain a reversion.

DESTRUCTIBILITY JURISDICTION: If Larry has not had a son by the time he dies, the contingent remainder would be "destroyed." Jack's reversion would then become possessory.

NON-DESTRUCTIBILITY JURISDICTION: The effect would be the same in a non-destructibility jurisdiction because, if Larry has not had a son by the time of his death, there is no possibility for a son to be born later (except, of course, in the case that Larry had frozen some of his sperm). Therefore, the condition can no longer be fulfilled; and the estate would pass to the holder of the next interest, in this case, Jack.

7.   Mr. Angelou ➜ Jack for life, then to Janet for life if she marries, then to Chrissy for 10
      years.

T	
SoT	

7.　　Mr. Angelou ➔ Jack for life, then to Janet for life if she marries, then to Chrissy for 10 years.

T	Mr. Angelou to Jack in <u>life estate</u>, then to Janet in <u>life estate</u> if she marries, then to Chrissy for <u>a term of years</u>	
SoT	Jack Janet Chrissy Mr. Angelou	- life estate - contingent remainder in life estate - vested remainder for a term of years - reversion

The words of purchase "to Jack" denote Jack as the grantee of the present possessory interest; thus, he receives the estate. The words of limitation "for life" identify the estate as a life estate.

The words of purchase "to Janet" denote Janet as the grantee of a future interest. The words of limitation "for life" identify the estate (that will exist if the future interest becomes possessory) as a life estate. The interest is a remainder because (i) it is capable of becoming possessory immediately upon the expiration of the preceding estate and (ii) it cannot divest any other interests. It is a contingent remainder because it is subject to the condition precedent that Janet marries.

The words of purchase "to Chrissy" denote Chrissy as the grantee of a future interest. The words of limitation "for 10 years" identify the estate (that will exist if the future interest becomes possessory) as a term of years (here, an estate of fixed duration lasting exactly 10 years). The interest is a remainder because (i) it is capable of becoming possessory immediately upon the expiration of the preceding estate and (ii) it cannot divest any other interests. It is vested because (i) Chrissy is ascertainable at the time of the conveyance [you can point to her] and (ii) there is no condition precedent.

Mr. Angelou holds a future interest known as a reversion. A reversion will always follow a contingent remainder because someone must always hold seisin . Since the contingent remainder is not certain to vest, the grantor must retain a reversion. When Chrissy's term of years ends, Mr. Angelou's reversion will become possessory.

DESTRUCTIBILITY JURISDICTION: If Janet is not married when Jack dies, her contingent remainder would be "destroyed," and she loses any and all interest in the estate. The estate would then pass to Chrissy.

NON-DESTRUCTIBILITY JURISDICTION: If Janet is not married when Jack dies, the estate would revert to the grantor, Mr. Angelou, to hold in fee simple on executory limitation until the condition is satisfied or until it is no longer capable of being performed (Janet's death). At this point, Janet's interest becomes a springing executory interest. It is an executory interest because it follows a fee simple on executory limitation; it is springing because Janet, a transferee, would divest Mr. Angelou, the transferor.

At Janet's death, Chrissy's interest will become possessory.

8.   Mr. Angelou ➔ Jack for life if he ever becomes a famous chef, then to Larry.

T	
SoT	

8.   Mr. Angelou ➔ Jack for life if he ever becomes a famous chef, then to Larry.

T	Mr. Angelou to Jack in <u>life estate</u> if he ever becomes a famous chef, then to Larry in <u>fee simple</u>	
SoT	Mr. Angelou	- fee simple on executory limitation
	Jack	- springing executory interest in life estate
	Larry	- vested remainder in fee simple

Mr. Angelou has present possession of the estate in fee simple. However, he will be divested of this estate if Jack becomes a famous chef. Therefore, Mr. Angelou has a fee simple on executory limitation. His interest will be cut short if Jack becomes a famous chef.

The words of purchase "to Jack" denote Jack as the grantee of an interest. The words of limitation "for life" identify the estate (that will exist if the future interest becomes possessory) as a life estate. However, the interest is subject to the condition that Jack becomes a famous chef before gaining possession of the estate. The interest is an executory interest because it is a future interest which follows a fee simple. It is a springing interest because Jack, a transferee, will divest Mr. Angelou, the transferor, of the estate. If Jack becomes a famous chef, he will receive the estate and divest Mr. Angelou's fee simple.

The words of purchase "to Larry" denote Larry as the grantee of a future interest. There are no words of limitation, so a fee simple is presumed. Larry's interest is a remainder because (i) it is capable of becoming possessory immediately upon the expiration of the preceding estate and (ii) it cannot divest any other interest. It is vested because (i) Larry is ascertainable at the time of the conveyance and (ii) there is no condition precedent.

DESTRUCTIBILITY JURISDICTION: Destructibility does not apply because there is no contingent remainder.

9. Larry ➔ Cindy for life, then to Mr. Ferley for life if he marries Mrs. Roper, then to Jack and the heirs of his body by Janet if Jack has a child.

T	
SoT	

9.   Larry ➜   Cindy for life, then to Mr. Ferley for life if he marries Mrs. Roper, then to Jack and the heirs of his body by Janet if Jack has a child.

T	Larry to Cindy in <u>life estate</u>, then to Mr. Ferley in <u>life estate</u> if he marries Mrs. Roper, then to Jack in <u>fee tail special</u> if Jack has a child
SoT	Cindy — life estate Mr. Ferley — contingent remainder in life estate Jack — contingent remainder in fee tail special Larry — reversion

The words of purchase "to Cindy" denote Cindy as the grantee of the present possessory interest; thus, she receives the estate. The words of limitation "for life" identify the estate as a life estate.

The words of purchase "to Mr. Ferley" denote Mr. Ferley as the grantee of a future interest. The words of limitation "for life" identify the estate (that will exist if the future interest becomes possessory) as a life estate. The interest is a remainder because (i) it is capable of becoming possessory immediately upon the expiration of the preceding estate and (ii) it cannot divest any other interests. It is a contingent remainder because it is subject to the condition precedent that Mr. Ferley marry Mrs. Roper.

The words of purchase "to Jack" denote Jack as the grantee of a future interest. The words of limitation "and the heirs of his body" identify the estate (that will exist if the future interest becomes possessory) as a fee tail. The interest is a remainder because (i) it is capable of becoming possessory immediately upon the expiration of the preceding estate and (ii) it cannot divest any other interests. It is a contingent remainder because it is subject to the condition precedent that Jack have a child by Janet.

Larry retains a future interest known as a reversion. A reversion will always follow a contingent remainder because someone must hold seisin in the estate at all times. Since a contingent remainder is not certain to vest, the grantor must retain a reversion.

DESTRUCTIBILITY JURISDICTION: If Mr. Ferley has not married Mrs. Roper by the time Cindy dies, his contingent remainder would be "destroyed," and he loses any and all interest in the estate.

If Jack has not had a child by the time Mr. Ferley dies [or, if Mr. Ferley's interest never vested, by the time of Cindy's death], then Jack's contingent remainder would be "destroyed," and he loses any and all interest in the estate. Larry's reversion would then become possessory.

NON-DESTRUCTIBILITY JURISDICTION: If Mr. Ferley has not married Mrs. Roper by the time Cindy dies, then the estate would revert to the grantor, Larry, to hold in fee simple on executory limitation until the condition is satisfied (Mr. Ferley marrying Mrs. Roper) or until it is no longer capable of being performed (Mr. Ferley's death). At this point, Mr. Ferley's interest becomes a springing executory interest. It is an executory interest because it follows a fee simple on executory limitation; it is springing because Mr. Ferley, a transferee, would divest Larry, the transferor.

If Jack has not had a child by the time Mr. Ferley dies [or, if Mr. Ferley's interest never vested, by the time of Cindy's death], then the estate would revert to the grantor, Larry, to hold in fee simple on executory limitation until the condition is satisfied or until it is no longer capable of being performed (Jack's death). At this point, Janet's interest becomes a springing executory interest (in fee tail special). It is an executory interest because it follows a fee simple on executory limitation; it is springing because Mr. Ferley, a transferee, would divest Larry, the transferor.

10.   Mr. Ferley ➔ Bart for life, then to Janet if she becomes a florist, but if not, then to Jack.

T	
SoT	

10. Mr. Ferley ➜ Bart for life, then to Janet if she becomes a florist, but if not, then to Jack.

T	Mr. Ferley to Bart in <u>life estate</u>, then to Janet in <u>fee simple</u> if she becomes a florist, **but if** not, then to Jack in <u>fee simple</u>	
SoT	Bart	- life estate
	Janet	- alternative contingent remainder in fee simple
	Jack	- alternative contingent remainder in fee simple
	Mr. Ferley	- reversion

The words of purchase "to Bart" denote Bart as the grantee of the present possessory interest; thus, he receives the estate. The words of limitation "for life" identify the estate as a life estate.

The words of purchase "to Janet" denote Janet as the grantee of a future interest. The words of limitation "and her heirs" identify the estate (that will exist if the future interest becomes possessory) as a fee simple. The interest is a remainder because (i) it is capable of becoming possessory immediately upon the expiration of the preceding estate and (ii) it cannot divest any other interests. It is a contingent remainder because it is subject to the condition precedent that Janet become a florist. The interest is an alternative contingent remainder because the grantor provided that, if the condition for vesting is not fulfilled by one grantee, the interest will vest in another grantee. If one vests, the other cannot. Janet's interest will vest and become possessory if she becomes a florist. If Janet does not become a florist, Jack's interest will vest.

The words of purchase "to Jack" denote Jack as the grantee of a future interest. The words of limitation "and his heirs" identify the estate (that will exist if the future interest becomes possessory) as a fee simple. The interest is a remainder because (i) it is capable of becoming possessory immediately upon the expiration of the preceding estate and (ii) it cannot divest any other interests. It is a contingent remainder because it is subject to the condition precedent that Janet does not become a florist. The interest is an alternative contingent remainder because the grantor provided that, if the condition for vesting is not fulfilled by one grantee, the interest will vest in another grantee. Jack's interest will vest if Janet's interest does not vest.

Mr. Ferley retains a future interest known as a reversion. A reversion will always follow a contingent remainder because someone must hold seisin in the estate at all times. Even though alternative contingent remainders are mutually exclusive and will exhaust all possibilities, the grantor is still deemed to retain a reversion.

DESTRUCTIBILITY JURISDICTION: If Janet is not a florist when Bart dies, her contingent remainder would be "destroyed," and she loses any and all interest in the estate. If Janet is a florist, then Jack's interest will be destroyed because there is no way his interest can vest after Janet's.

[NOTE: Alternative Continent Remainders are designed so as to prevent non-vesting contingent remainders from remaining. This means that no matter what jurisdiction you are in, if you have alternative continent remainders, one interest will automatically be destroyed].

NON-DESTRUCTIBILITY JURISDICTION: Since the contingent remainders created in this conveyance are alternative contingent remainders, the one which does not vest will be destroyed even in a non-destructibility jurisdiction. In this case, either Janet's or Jack's interest will be lost when the other one vests.

Rule Against Perpetuities

Wealth and power in Anglo-American society have long been measured by the ownership of land. The ability of land to be devised or inherited allows wealth and power to be concentrated within a particular family group. A person wishing to preserve her family's wealth after her death might include provisions in her will that would operate to control the disposition of her wealth for many generations. Such will provisions were designed to keep land in family hands and favor the "blood" for generations to come.

These restrictions upon the alienation of property were completely contrary to notions favoring free exchange. Historically, "dead hand" restrictions on alienability caused inefficient land use and the wasting of valuable resources. The common law fought back by developing the Doctrine of Destructibility of Contingent Remainders and the Rule Against Perpetuities.

The Rule Against Perpetuities is not intuitive. Common formulations of the Rule are confusing and obscure. Yet the Rule is deceptively simple. Its most common version reads:

> No interest is good unless it must vest, if at all, not later than 21 years after some life in being at the creation of the interest.

In short, an interest that might vest after "a life in being plus 21 years" (the perpetuities period) is invalid. Invalid interests are "blue-penciled" out of the conveyance ab initio (at the time of conveyance). It is as if these interests were never created. The remaining parts of the conveyance are left intact.

The Rule is only concerned with when an interest will vest in interest. An interest vests in interest when there are no longer any conditions precedent required to fix or guarantee its enjoyment. An interest can be vested in interest even when the right of enjoyment (physical possession) cannot be exercised until an unknown time in the future. This unknown period of time may delay the possessory enjoyment of the interest (i.e., delay the interest from becoming vested in possession), but it cannot prevent the interest from becoming possessory eventually. For purposes of the Rule, it is irrelevant when an interest will vest in possession. Consider the following example:

Ex: Casey ➔ Gish for life, then to Jon if Jon reaches 95.

Facts: Gish and Jon are alive; Jon is 18 and in poor health.

T	Casey to Gish in <u>life estate</u>, then to Jon in <u>fee simple</u> if Jon reaches 95
SoT	Gish - life estate Jon - contingent remainder in fee simple Casey - reversion

The words of purchase "to Gish" denote Gish as the grantee of a present possessory interest; thus, he receives the estate. The words of limitation "for life" identify the estate as a life estate.

The words of purchase "to Jon" denote Jon as the grantee of a future interest. There are no words of limitation, so a fee simple is presumed. Jon's future interest is a remainder because it is capable of becoming possessory immediately upon the expiration of the preceding estate and it cannot divest any other interests. It is a contingent remainder in interest because it is subject to the condition precedent that Jon reaches 95. When Jon turns 95, his remainder becomes vested in interest because he will have satisfied the condition precedent. However, Jon's remainder will not become vested in possession until Gish's death.

What interests are subject to RAP?

The interests that are subject to the Rule are future interests that have not vested in interest. For our purposes, there are three types: contingent remainders, executory interests, and vested remainders subject to open (subject to divestment). Interests which are not subject to the Rule are present possessory interests and future interests in the grantor (reversions, possibilities of reverter, and rights of entry), all of which are deemed to be vested in interest for purposes of the Rule.

Elements of RAP

> No interest is good unless:
>
> (i) it must vest, if at all,
>
> (ii) not later than 21 years after some life in being at the creation of the interest

(i) it must vest, if at all

It is important to emphasize that the future interest might never vest. RAP does not require the interest to vest within the perpetuities period -- only that if it does vest, it must vest within the perpetuities period. Therefore, in the above conveyance [Casey to Gish for life, then to Jon if he reaches 95], Jon's contingent remainder does not violate RAP even though it is quite likely that Jon's interest will never vest in possession (he never reaches 95). We do know with certainty that if the interest ever vests, it must vest during Jon's lifetime (Jon must be alive to reach his 95th birthday).

(ii) ...not later than 21 years after some life in being at the creation of the interest

(a) "not later than 21 years" defines the perpetuities period. It is measured by adding 21 years to the time the last "life in being" dies. In the above example, if Casey died in 1975, Gish in 1989, and Jon in 1995, the perpetuities period would be measured by adding 21 years to 1995 (Jon's death) – i.e., through 2016. But traditional RAP does not wait and see what actually happens (i.e., who dies when); it demands that you hypothetically analyze all possibilities that can affect vesting. The easiest way to structure your analysis is to kill off all lives in being together at some point in the future (see below).

Note, government entities, partnerships, and corporations are not considered to be "lives in being" because they have potentially infinite existence.

(b) a "life in being" is someone who has already been born, or conceived, at the time the interest is created. Theoretically, a life in being can be anyone in the world born or conceived at the time of creation of the interest. To simplify matters, treat as "lives in being" any party named in, or implicated by, the conveyance. Therefore, Casey, Gish, and Jon would be the "lives in being".

Traditionally, a child conceived, but not born, before the grantor's death is considered to be alive from the time of conception.

(c) "at the creation of the interest" refers to a single moment in time: (i) in the case of an inter vivos transfer, when the deed (or property) is delivered; or (ii) in the case of a will, when the testator dies.

Putting the pieces together, (i) for an inter vivos conveyance, the perpetuities period is 21 years from the death of the last person who had been born or conceived at the time the grantor delivered the deed or property; and (ii) for a conveyance created in a will, the perpetuities period is 21 years from the death of the last person who had been born or conceived at the time of the testator's death.

RAP as a rule of proof

RAP can be viewed as a rule of proof. In this setting, your primary task is to demonstrate either (i) that the applicable future interest must vest, if at all, within the perpetuities period (the interest is good); or conversely, (ii) that there is at least one possibility of remote vesting (the interest is void). Seen in this way, RAP can be rephrased:

If there is any possibility that an applicable future interest will vest in interest more than 21 years from the death of the lives in being at the creation of the interest, the future interest is invalid.

Remember, RAP limits the period of time between the creation of the future interest and its vesting in interest. When it actually vests in possession is irrelevant; that it might vest within the perpetuities period is irrelevant; that it may vest too remotely is the key. For purposes of developing your proof, use all lives in being named or implicated by the grant.

A RAP Checklist

1. Identify the interests created by the conveyance.

2. Note if any of the interests are contingent remainders, executory interests, or vested remainders subject to open.

3. List the lives in being at the creation of interest.

4. Give birth to any after-born persons.

5. Kill off all of the lives in being (at creation) at some future point and add 21 years from this date (the "RAP line").

6. Ask: Is there any possibility that the interest will vest beyond the "RAP line"?

    •   If it is possible that the interest may vest after this date (the RAP line), it is invalid. Strike the interest.

    •   If the interest must vest, if at all, within the "RAP line" (i.e., it cannot possibly vest remotely), it is valid.

Applying RAP correctly requires imagination. One begins with the facts as they exist at the time of the conveyance; but one must also imagine possibilities that could arise in the future that may affect vesting. It does not matter how many different ways an interest might vest before the "RAP line" (the death of the last life in being plus 21 years). Indeed, there may be millions of such possibilities. If it is possible to conceive of just one fact pattern where the interest vests after the "RAP line" (death of the last life in being plus 21 years), the interest is invalid. All possibilities should be taken into account.

Illustration #1

Ex: Stan ➔ Cartman and his heirs, but if it is not used as a school, to Kenny and his heirs.

T	Stan to Cartman in <u>fee simple</u>, **but if** it is not used as a school to Kenny in <u>fee simple</u>	
SoT	Cartman	- fee simple on executory limitation
	Kenny	- shifting executory interest in fee simple

RAP is violated. The interests really are:

M(RAP)	Cartman	- fee simple
	Kenny	- nothing

1.   Identify the interests

The words of purchase "to Cartman" denote Cartman as the grantee of the present possessory interest; thus, he receives the estate. The words of limitation "and his heirs" identify the estate as a fee simple. However, the words "but if" are words of divestment that create a defeasible fee. Since the defeasible fee is followed by an interest in a third party, Cartman has a fee simple on executory limitation.

The words of purchase "to Kenny" denote Kenny as the grantee of a future interest. The words of limitation "and his heirs" identify the estate as a fee simple. Since a future interest in a third party follows a defeasible fee, Kenny's future interest is an executory interest in fee simple. It is a shifting interest because Kenny, a transferee, could divest Cartman, another transferee, of the estate.

2.   Note the contingent remainders, executory interests, and vested remainders subject to open

The Rule must be tested against Kenny's shifting executory interest. Cartman's fee simple defeasible is a present possessory interest and therefore is deemed to be vested in interest for purposes of the Rule.

3.   List the lives in being

Stan, Cartman and Kenny are all alive at the time of the conveyance and can be treated as lives in being.

4.   Give birth to any potential afterborns that might affect vesting

Suppose that in early 2009 Cartman has a grandchild, Wendy (and therefore she is not a life in being at creation of the interest). Kenny also has a grandchild, Bebe, in early 2009.

5.   Kill the lives in being and add 21 years

In late 2010, Stan, Cartman, and Kenny go hunting with Jimbo. Jimbo mistakes Kenny for an endangered bird and shoots him. [Oh no...Jimbo killed Kenny!) Stan and Cartman try to rescue Kenny, but instead they fall off the mountain and die. Therefore, 2031 becomes the "RAP line".

6.   Is there any possibility of remote vesting (that it will cease to be used as a playground past 2031)?

Is there any possibility that the executory interest may vest more than 21 years after Stan, Cartman and Kenny die (past the 2031 "RAP line")? One possibility: In early 2009, Wendy, Cartman's granddaughter, is born (she is not a life in being at creation). Stan, Cartman, and Kenny all die in late 2010. After Cartman dies, Wendy takes possession of Southacre. Thirty years later (in 2040), tired of hearing children screaming, Wendy throws out the school and converts the property into a wildlife preserve. Kenny's successor, Bebe, steps forward to seize Southacre, claiming the condition precedent to their executory interest has occurred, and their interest has vested. Since their interest vests more than 21 years after the deaths of all lives in being (after the 2031 "RAP line"), RAP has been violated. [Note, Kenny's early death has little significance; it is the executory interest that remains our focus. Kenny is merely the initial holder of the interest; when he dies, it goes to his devisees or heirs.]

When a conveyance violates the Rule Against Perpetuities, it does so ab initio, at the moment of its creation. Remember, at common law, RAP deals with what might happen in the future. It does not care what actually happens or what is most likely to happen. The traditional solution is to blue-pencil out (strike) the part of the conveyance creating the interest that violates the Rule. In this case, the executory interest in Kenny violates the Rule. This future interest is struck. Therefore, after applying RAP, the conveyance reads: "Stan ➔ Cartman and his heirs." [Note, the phrase "but if it is not used as a playground" is considered part of the executory interest.] Cartman has a fee simple. Kenny gets nothing.

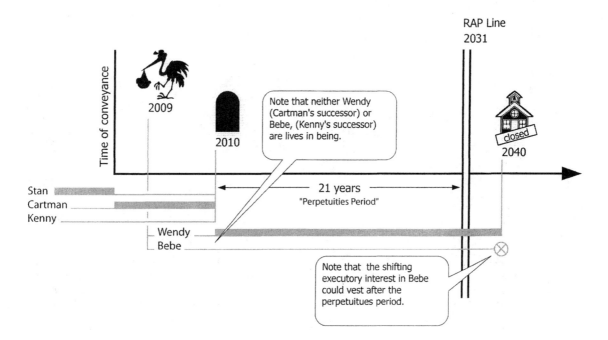

Illustration #2

Ex: Kyle ➔ Kenny for life, then to the first child of Chef who reaches 23.

Facts: Kenny is alive. Chef is alive and has two children, Ike who is 3, and Stan who is 20.

T	Kyle to Kenny in <u>life estate</u>, then to the first child of Chef who reaches 23 in <u>fee simple</u>	
SoT	Kenny First child to reach 23 Kyle	- life estate - contingent remainder in fee simple - reversion

RAP is violated. The interests really are:

M(RAP)	Kenny Kyle	- life estate - reversion

1.   Identify the Interests

The words of purchase "to Kenny" denote Kenny as the grantee of the present possessory interest; thus, he receives the estate. The words of limitation "for life" identify the estate as a life estate.

The words of purchase "to the first child of Chef to reach 23" denote the grantee of a future interest. There are no words of limitation, so a fee simple is presumed. The first child of Chef to reach 23 has a remainder because the interest is capable of becoming possessory immediately upon the expiration of the preceding estate and it cannot divest any other interests. It is a contingent remainder because "the first child of Chef who reaches 23" is presently unascertainable.

Kyle retains a future interest known as a reversion. A reversion will always follow a contingent remainder because someone must hold seisin in the estate at all times. Since a contingent remainder is not certain to vest, the grantor must retain a reversion. The reversion will become possessory if Chef has no children who reach 23.

2.   Note the contingent remainders, executory interests, and vested remainders subject to open

The Rule must be tested against the contingent remainder. Kenny's life estate and Kyle's reversion (respectively, a present possessory interest and a future interest in the grantor) are deemed to be vested for purposes of the Rule.

3.   List the lives in being

Kyle, Kenny, Chef and Chef's children, Ike and Stan, were all born and ascertainable when the conveyance was made. Therefore, they are all lives in being at the creation of the interest.

4.   Give birth to any potential afterborns that might affect vesting

Chef could give birth to another child, Cartman, in 2009. If Chef has another child AFTER the conveyance, that child is NOT a life in being for the purposes of the Rule (since the child was not alive at the time of conveyance). Note, even if Chef was of an age considered to be beyond fertility, at common law he still is considered capable of conceiving a child; he also could adopt.

5.   Kill the lives in being and add 21 years

In 2010 a huge snow storm hits South Park. Kyle, Kenny, Chef, Ike and Stan are all trapped in a cabin in the mountains and die of starvation in 2010. Therefore, 2031 becomes the "RAP line".

6. Is there any possibility of remote vesting (can a child of Chef reach 23 past 2031)?

Does any child of Chef have the possibility of becoming "the first child of Chef to reach 23" more than 21 years after Kyle, Kenny, Chef, Ike and Stan die (after the 2031 "RAP line")? Yes. Cartman (not a life in being at the creation of the interest) will become 23 in 2032, one year after the perpetuities period; it would vest more than 21 years after the death of all the lives in being at the creation of the interest.

When a conveyance violates the Rule Against Perpetuities, it does so ab initio, at the moment of its creation. The common law's traditional solution was to strike out the part of the conveyance creating the interest that violates the Rule. In this case, the contingent remainder is "Chef's first child to reach 23". This future interest is struck. Therefore, the conveyance after the application of RAP reads: "Kyle → Kenny for life." Kenny has a life estate. Since Kyle did not convey his entire estate, Kyle retains a reversion. RAP only applies to contingent remainders, executory interests, and vested remainders subject to open. RAP never applies to reversions. Ike and Stan get nothing.

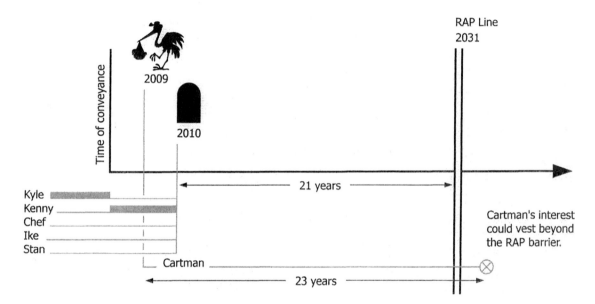

Modern Applications of RAP

Many jurisdictions have reformed the Rule Against Perpetuities by adopting one or both of the following doctrines: (i) Wait-and-See; or (ii) Cy Pres.

Wait-and-See:

Some jurisdictions will only invalidate an interest if it actually vests after "lives in being plus 21 years". The legitimacy of an interest is judged not at the time the interest is created but at the time that the interest vests or has failed to vest. Only if the interest actually fails to vest within "lives in being plus 21 years" is it invalid. Thus, under wait-and-see, we look not at far ranging legal possibilities, but at the actually occurring realities that follow the conveyance.

In Illustration 2, a wait-and-see jurisdiction may validate the contingent remainder, depending on what actually occurs in the individuals lives. As one example, if Stan becomes 23 before Kenny (a life in being) dies, the contingent remainder is a valid interest (and, at that moment, becomes vested).

Changing the facts -- suppose Chef did have another child, Cartman, in 2000. Since the contingent remainder could vest after 21 years of the death of the last life in being (see above), the interest was void when applying traditional RAP principles. In a wait-and-wee jurisdiction, we let the facts play out to see what happens. If Chef dies (with all the other lives in being) when Cartman is 10 years old (in 2010) and Chef has no other children, the contingent remainder is valid. Since the perpetuities period begins at Chef's actual death (rather than at some hypothetical date), Cartman's interest, if it is going to vest, will vest in 13 years (Cartman will become 23, if at all, 13 years after Chef's death - since he is now 10). The Rule cannot possibly be violated.

Uniform Statutory Rule Against Perpetuities ("USRAP")

USRAP is similar to the wait and see approach, but rather than applying the traditional period of twenty-one years, USRAP jurisdictions apply a ninety (90) year period (after the death of all lives in being). An interest is valid if it satisfies traditional RAP or if the interest actually vests within the ninety year period.

Cy Pres:

When the conveyance of an interest would violate traditional RAP principles, some jurisdictions may allow the courts to reform the conveyance so that it no longer violates the Rule. The court rewrites the conveyance "as near as possible" to the grantor's original intent. Cy Pres can only be used by the court if it is convinced that the rewriting will be consistent with the grantor's original, general goals. For example, a contingent interest in an unborn person that becomes vested when the person reaches 23 might be changed so that the interest becomes vested when the person reaches the age of 21. [Some states combine the two reforms, observing a Wait-and-See period and allowing for judicial reformation at the end of the period if the interest fails to vest.]

Cy Pres is a judicial tool for reforming a conveyance in a manner consistent with the intentions of the grantor. A judge in applying this doctrine should not engage in fantasy or idle speculation.

In Illustration 2 above, a court in a jurisdiction applying cy pres may forward the following analysis:

> "the contingent remainder violated RAP because of the possibility that another child could be born who would reach the age of 23 after Kyle, Kenny, Chef, Ike and Stan died and 21 years passed. But evidence presented gives us confidence that Kyle (the grantor) wanted a child of Chef to receive the estate. We will apply cy pres and reform the conveyance to read: "Kyle ➔ Kenny for life, then to the first child of Chef who reaches 21."

By simply reducing the age at which the interest vests by two years (to 21), any interest in a child of Chef, alive now, or born after, the conveyance is good (with respect to the Rule Against Perpetuities).

Rule Against Perpetuities Problems

1.   Mr. Garrison ➔ Kenny for life, then to Kenny's first child to reach 30 and his heirs.

Facts: Kenny has no children.

T	
SoT	

M(RAP)	

1. Mr. Garrison ➜ Kenny for life, then to Kenny's first child to reach 30 and his heirs.

    Facts: Kenny has no children.

T	Mr. Garrison to Kenny in <u>life estate</u>, then to Kenny's first child to reach 30 in <u>fee simple</u>
SoT	Kenny - life estate Kenny's first child to reach 30 - contingent remainder in fee simple Mr. Garrison - reversion

Kenny's first child's interest violates RAP. The interests should read:

M(RAP)	Kenny - life estate Mr. Garrison - reversion

The words of purchase "to Kenny" denote Kenny as the grantee of the present possessory interest; thus, he receives the estate. The words of limitation "for life" identify the estate as a life estate.

The words of purchase "to Kenny's first child to reach 30" denote the grantee of a future interest. The words of limitation "and his heirs" identify the estate (that will exist if the future interest becomes possessory) as a fee simple. The interest is a remainder because (i) it is capable of becoming possessory immediately upon the expiration of the preceding estate and (ii) it cannot divest any other interests. It is a contingent remainder because, at the time of the conveyance, the child is unascertainable and it is subject to the condition precedent that the child reach 30. If a child of Kenny reaches 30, the remainder will vest.

Mr. Garrison retains a future interest known as a reversion. A reversion will always follow a contingent remainder since someone must hold seisin in the estate at all times. Since a contingent remainder is not certain to vest, the grantor must retain a reversion. Mr. Garrison's reversion will vest if no child of Kenny's reaches 30.

2. Note the contingent remainders, executory interests, and vested remainders subject to open

The Rule must be tested against the contingent reminder of "Kenny's first child to reach 30". Kenny's present possessory life estate and Mr. Garrison's reversion are deemed to be vested for purposes of the Rule.

3. List the lives in being

Mr. Garrison and Kenny are both alive at the time of the conveyance and can be treated as the lives in being.

4. Give birth to any potential afterborns that might affect vesting

Kenny could have a child (or children) after the conveyance. Kenny may have a child, Pip, in 2009. If Kenny has a child AFTER the conveyance, that child is NOT a life in being for the purposes of the Rule.

5. Kill off the lives in being and add 21 years

Suppose that in 2010 Kenny slips in the snow, falls into Mr. Garrison, and the two of them meet an untimely end. The lives in being are now dead. The 'RAP line" becomes 2031.

6. Is there any possibility of remote vesting (that Pip will reach 30 past 2031)?

Is there any possibility that the contingent remainder may vest more than 21 years after all lives in being (Kenny and Mr. Garrison) die (past the 2031 "RAP line")? One possibility: Pip is born in 2009. In 2010 Kenny and Mr. Garrison die. Pip lives for another 30 years. The contingent remainder vests in 2040 (2010 + 30). Since Pip's interest vests more than 21 years after the deaths of all lives in being (after the 2031 "RAP line"), RAP has been violated.

When a conveyance violates the Rule Against Perpetuities, it does so when it is made, not 21 years later. The interest is void ab initio, from the moment that it is created. In the absence of reform tools, the offending interest is struck. Hence, the contingent remainder in Kenny's first child to reach 30 is blue-penciled out. The conveyance now reads:

Mr. Garrison ➔ Kenny for life.

Kenny has a life estate. Mr. Garrison has a reversion. Kenny's first child to reach 30 gets nothing.

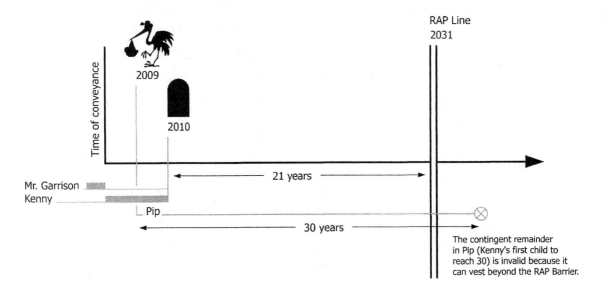

Modern Applications:

If the conveyance violates the traditional Rule, look at it one more time. Check to see if you are in a jurisdiction that: (i) looks to what actually happens during the perpetuities period applicable to the interest (Wait-and-See Doctrine); or (ii) permits reformation of the conveyance (Cy Pres Doctrine). If so, the conveyance may be saved.

Wait-and-See Jurisdiction: Wait until the end of the perpetuities period (lives in being plus 21 years). If at this point in time the interest has vested, it is good. However, if it has not yet vested, the interest fails. Using this approach, we would wait 21 years after Kenny's death to see if Pip's interest had vested. In this example, Pip would only be 21, so his interest would fail because there is a possibility of vesting in 9 years. However, if the facts were slightly different and Kenny did not die until Pip was 15, then at the end of 21 years, Pip's interest would have already vested (so it would be saved).

Cy Pres Jurisdiction: The court can rewrite the conveyance consistent with the grantor's general intentions. If Cy Pres is utilized, the conveyance might read:

Mr. Garrison ➔ Kenny for life, then to Kenny's first child to reach 21 and his heirs.

2.   Jimbo ➜ My first relative and his heirs to shoot an endangered bird.

T	
SoT	

M(RAP)	

2.   Jimbo ➜ My first relative and his heirs to shoot an endangered bird.

T	Jimbo to my first relative in <u>fee simple</u> to shoot an endangered bird
SoT	Jimbo - fee simple on executory limitation 1st relative to shoot … - springing executory interest in fee simple

RAP has been violated. The interest is void.

M(RAP)	Jimbo retains his fee simple.

The words of purchase "to my first relative to shoot an endangered bird" denote the grantee of an estate. The words of limitation "and his heirs" identify the estate as a fee simple. However, the conveyance states a condition which must occur prior to the relative gaining possession; therefore, the relative's interest is a future interest. Because the future interest will divest the grantor of the estate, the interest is an executory interest. It is a springing executory interest because the relative, a transferee, will divest Jimbo, the transferor, of the estate. Jimbo's first relative to shoot an endangered bird will get the estate.

Jimbo has present possession of the estate. He holds a fee simple on executory limitation (subject to divestment). His interest will be cut short if one of his relatives shoots an endangered bird.

2. Note the contingent remainders, executory interests, and vested remainders subject to open

The Rule must be tested against the executory interest. Jimbo's present possessory fee simple on executory limitation is a vested estate and not subject to the Rule.

3. List the lives in being

Jimbo and all his relatives living at the time of the conveyance are lives in being

4. Give birth to any potential afterborns that might affect vesting

A child could be born to Jimbo or one of Jimbo's living relatives (and thereby become a relative of Jimbo) shortly after the conveyance. Suppose Timmy, the son of Jimbo's cousin, is born in early 2009.

5. Kill the lives in being and add 21 years

Suppose that in late 2010 Jimbo and "all living relatives at the time of conveyance" die in a common disaster. The lives in being are now dead. The "RAP line" becomes 2031.

6. Is there any possibility of remote vesting (that Timmy will kill an endangered bird sometime past 2031)?

Is there any possibility that the executory interest may vest more than 21 years after all lives in being (Jimbo and his relatives living at the time of the conveyance) die (past the 2031 "RAP line")? One possibility: Since Timmy was born after the conveyance he is not a life in being. Timmy becomes a hunter at age forty and shoots an endangered bird in 2050. The executory interest vests in 2050, far beyond the 2031 "RAP line"). RAP has been violated.

When a conveyance violates the Rule Against Perpetuities, it does so when it is made, not 21 years later. The interest is void ab initio, from the moment that it is created. In the absence of reform tools, the offending interest is struck. In this case, there would be no interest created. Jimbo retains his fee simple absolute.

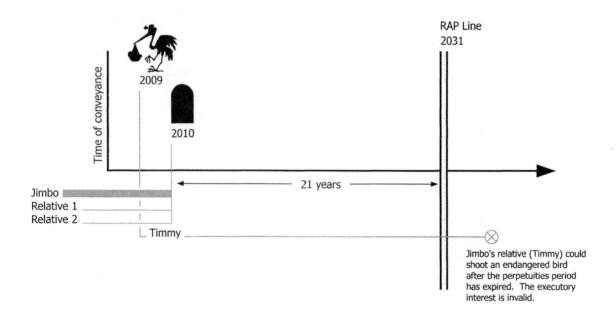

Jimbo's relative (Timmy) could shoot an endangered bird after the perpetuities period has expired. The executory interest is invalid.

Modern Applications of RAP:

If the conveyance violates the traditional Rule, look at it one more time. Check to see if you are in a jurisdiction that: (i) looks to what actually happens during the perpetuities period applicable to the interest (Wait-and-See Doctrine); or (ii) permits reformation of the conveyance (Cy Pres Doctrine). If so, the conveyance may be saved.

Wait-and-See Jurisdiction: Wait until the end of the perpetuities period (lives in being plus 21 years). If at this point in time the interest has vested, it is good. However, if it has not yet vested, the interest fails. Using this approach, we would wait 21 years after the last of Jimbo or his relatives (living at the time of the conveyance) to die and see if any relative's interest had vested. In this example, if a relative of Jimbo's has shot an endangered bird within 21 years after the last of Jimbo or his relatives (living at the time of the conveyance) to die, he would take the estate in fee simple absolute.

Cy Pres jurisdiction: The court can rewrite the conveyance consistent with the grantor's general intentions. If Cy Pres is utilized, the conveyance might read:

Jimbo ➔ My first relative now living to shoot an endangered bird.

[The conveyance is now limited to vesting, if at all, to someone who is a life in being ("now living").]

3.   Mr. Mackie ➜ Cartman for life, then to Kenny if Kenny lives to be 50.

T	
SoT	

M(RAP)	

3.   Mr. Mackie ➔ Cartman for life, then to Kenny if Kenny lives to be 50.

T	Mr. Mackie to Cartman in <u>life estate</u>, then to Kenny in <u>fee simple</u> if Kenny lives to be 50
SoT	Cartman - life estate Kenny - contingent remainder in fee simple Mr. Mackie - reversion

M(RAP)	RAP is not violated.

The words of purchase "to Cartman" denote Cartman as the grantee of the present possessory interest; thus, he receives the estate. The words of limitation "for life" identify the estate as a life estate.

The words of purchase "to Kenny" denote Kenny as the grantee of a future interest. There are no words of limitation, so a fee simple is presumed. The interest is a remainder because (i) it is capable of becoming possessory immediately upon the expiration of the preceding estate and (ii) it cannot divest any other interests. It is a contingent remainder because it is subject to the condition precedent that Kenny lives to be 50 years old.

Mr. Mackie retains a future interest known as a reversion. A reversion will always follow a contingent remainder because someone must hold seisin in the estate at all times. Since a contingent remainder is not certain to vest, the grantor must retain a reversion. Mr. Mackie's reversion becomes possessory if Kenny fails to live to be 50.

2.   Note the contingent remainders, executory interests, and vested remainders subject to open

The Rule must be tested against the contingent remainder of Kenny. Cartman's life estate, and Mr. Mackie's reversion (respectively, a present possessory interest and a future interest in the grantor) are deemed to be vested for purposes of the Rule.

3.   List the lives in being

Mr. Mackie, Cartman and Kenny are all alive at the time of conveyance. Therefore, they are all lives in being.

4.   Give birth to any potential afterborns that might affect vesting

No children, issue, heirs, or widows are referred to in the conveyance. Afterborns need not be considered.

5.   Kill the lives in being and add 21 years

Suppose that Mr. Mackie, Cartman and Kenny die in late 2010. The lives in being are now dead. The "RAP line" becomes 2031.

6.   Is there any possibility of remote vesting (that Kenny will become 50 after he dies)?

Is there any possibility that the contingent remainder may vest more than 21 years after all lives in being (Mr. Mackie, Cartman, and Kenny) die? No. On thing is certain – Kenny will reach 50 during his lifetime, if at all. He may never reach 50; but remember the test is that the interest cannot vest after the last life in being plus 21 years. It does not have to vest to be a valid interest under the Rule.

Kenny's interest will either vest or fail to vest when Kenny dies (either Kenny lives to be 50 or he does not). In either case, since Kenny is a life in being at the creation of the interest, he will attain 50 or not during his life. There is no possibility of remote vesting. The contingent remainder cannot vest after Kenny's death; therefore, it does not violate RAP.

One would think that the possibility of a 50 year contingency period must be the kind of dead hand control that RAP was designed to prevent. But look closely. Remember, the critical period is measured from the death of the last life in being at the creation of the interest. The duration of a contingent interest alone is not the measure of the perpetuities period.

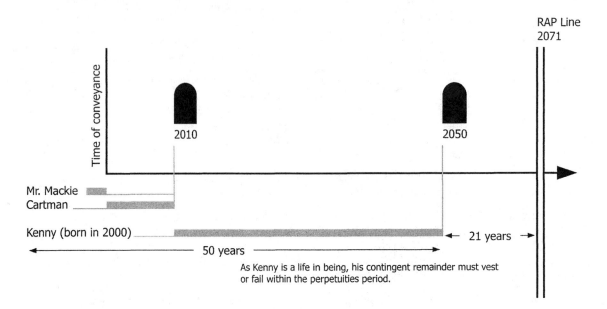

As Kenny is a life in being, his contingent remainder must vest or fail within the perpetuities period.

4. Cartman ➔ Kenny for life, then to Kenny's first child to reach 30.

      Facts: Cartman made this provision in a will he wrote in 2000. Cartman died in 2005, Kenny was alive and had no children.

T	
SoT	

M(RAP)	

4.   Cartman ➜ Kenny for life, then to Kenny's first child to reach 30.

Facts: Cartman made this provision in a will he wrote in 2000. Cartman died in 2005 (the time when the will becomes legally operative). Kenny was alive and had no children.

T	Cartman to Kenny in <u>life estate</u>, then to Kenny's first child to reach 30 in <u>fee simple</u>
SoT	Kenny - life estate Kenny's first child to reach 30 - contingent remainder in fee simple Cartman's heirs - reversion

The contingent remainder to Kenny's first child to reach 30 violates RAP. The interests should read:

M(RAP)	Kenny - life estate Cartman' heirs - reversion

The words of purchase "to Kenny" denote Kenny as the grantee of the present possessory interest; thus, he receives the estate. The words of limitation "for life" identify the estate as a life estate.

The words of purchase "to Kenny's first child to reach 30" denote the grantee of a future interest. There are no words of limitation, so a fee simple is presumed. The interest is a remainder because (i) it is capable of becoming possessory immediately upon the expiration of the preceding estate and (ii) it cannot divest any other interests. It is a contingent remainder because, at the time of the conveyance, Kenny's first child to reach 30 is unascertainable [you cannot point to him].

2.   Note the contingent remainders, executory interests, and vested remainders subject to open

The Rule must be tested against the contingent remainder of "Kenny's first child to reach 30".

3.   List the lives in being

Kenny is alive and ascertainable when the conveyance is made (since this is a will and consequently legally operative only at Cartman's death, Cartman is not a life in being).

4.   Give birth to any potential afterborns that can affect vesting

Kenny may have a child, Kyle, in early 2009, four years after Cartman dies (the time when the will becomes legally operative).

5.   Kill the lives in being and add 21 years

In late 2010 Kenny dies. The life in being is now dead. The "RAP line" becomes 2031.

6.   Is there any possibility of remote vesting (that Kyle will reach 30 past 2031)?

Is there any possibility that the contingent remainder may vest more than 21 years after the last life in being (Kenny) dies (past the 2031 "RAP line")? One possibility: Kyle is born in 2009. One year later Kenny dies. Kyle lives for another 30 years. The contingent remainder vests in 2039 (2009 + 30). Since Kyle's interest vests more than 21 years after the deaths of all lives in being (after the 2031 "RAP line"), RAP has been violated.

When an interest violates the Rules Against Perpetuities, it does so at its inception, not 21 years later. The interest is void ab initio, from the moment that it is created. In the absence of reform tools, the offending interest is struck. Hence, the contingent remainder in Kenny's first child to reach 30 is blue-penciled out. The conveyance (by will) now reads:

Cartman ➜ Kenny for life

Kenny has a life estate. Cartman's heirs or devisees retain a reversion (since Cartman is dead, he cannot hold the reversion).

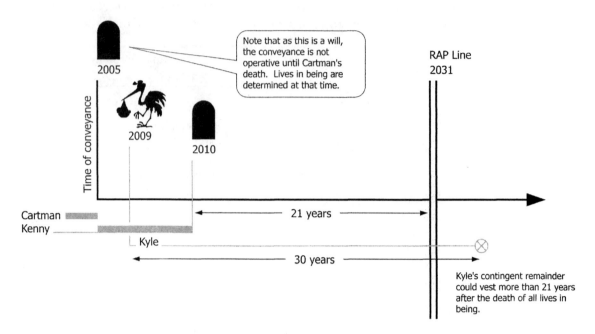

Modern Applications of RAP:

If the conveyance violates the traditional Rule, look at it one more time. Check to see if you are in a jurisdiction that: (i) looks to what actually happens during the perpetuities period applicable to the interest (Wait-and-See Doctrine); or (ii) permits reformation of the conveyance (Cy Pres Doctrine). If so, the conveyance may be saved.

Wait-and-See Jurisdiction: Wait until the end of the perpetuities period (lives in being plus 21 years). If at this point in time the interest has vested, it is good. However, if it has not yet vested, the interest fails. Using this approach, we would wait 21 years after Kenny's death to see if a child of Kenney has reached 21.

Cy Pres Jurisdiction: The court can rewrite the conveyance consistent with the grantor's general intentions. If cy pres is utilized, the conveyance might read:

Cartman ➔ Kenny for life, then to Kenny's first child to reach 21 and his heirs.

5.　　　Stan ➔ The City of South Park, its successors and assigns, but if the land is not used as a school, then to Kenny and his heirs if Kenny is then alive.

T	
SoT	

M(RAP)	

5.   Stan ➔ The City of South Park, its successors and assigns, but if the land is not used as a school, then to Kenny and his heirs if Kenny is then alive.

T	Stan to South Park in <u>fee simple</u>, **but if** the land is not used as a school, then to Kenny in <u>fee simple</u> if Kenny is then alive
SoT	South Park - fee simple on executory limitation Kenny - shifting executory interest in fee simple

M(RAP)	RAP is not violated.

The words of purchase "to South Park" denote South Park as the grantee of the present possessory interest; thus, the City receives the estate. The words of limitation "its successors and assigns" identify the estate as a fee simple. However, the words "but if" are words of limitation that create a defeasible fee. Since the defeasible fee is followed by an interest in a third party, the City has a fee simple on executory limitation.

The words of purchase "to Kenny" denote Kenny as the grantee of a future interest. The words of limitation "and his heirs" identify Kenny's interest (that will exist if the future interest becomes possessory) as a fee simple. Since the City's defeasible fee is followed by an interest in a third party, Kenny's interest is an executory interest. It is a shifting interest because Kenny, a transferee, will divest South Park, another transferee. However, the clause "if Kenny is then alive" creates a condition that further limits Kenny's interests. Kenny can only gain possession of the estate if he is alive at the time the land ceases to be used as a school.

2.   Note the contingent remainders, executory interests, and vested remainders subject to open

The Rule must be tested against Kenny's executory interest. South Park's fee simple on executory limitation (a present possessory interest) is deemed to be vested for purposes of the Rule.

3.   List the lives in being

Stan and Kenny were both alive at the time of the conveyance. Therefore, they are both lives in being. Remember, a life in being must be a real person. Thus, the City of South Park is not considered a life in being.

4.   Give birth to any potential afterborns

No children, issue, heirs, or widows are referred to in the conveyance. Afterborns need not be considered.

5.   Kill the lives in being and add 21 years

Suppose that Stan and Kenny both die in 2010. The lives in being are now dead. The "RAP line" becomes 2031.

6.   Is there any possibility of remote vesting (that Kyle will reach 30 past 2031)?

Is there any possibility that the executory interest may vest more than 21 years after the lives in being (Stan and Kenny) die (past the 2031 "RAP line")? No. Because Kenny's interest is contingent on his being alive, his interest cannot possibly vest after his death, let alone 21 years later. Can anyone else satisfy the condition and acquire a possessory interest in the estate more than 21 years after Kenny dies? No, it is limited to Kenny's lifetime. The interest will either vest in Kenny during his life or not. The conveyance does not violate RAP.

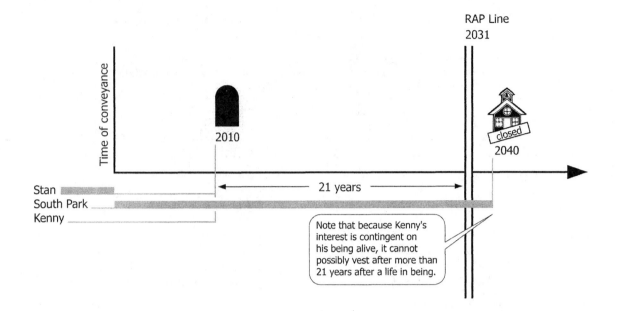

6. Stan ➔ the City of South Park, its successors and assigns, but if the land is not used as a park, then to Kenny and his heirs.

T	
SoT	

M(RAP)	

6.   Stan ➔ the City of South Park, its successors and assigns, but if the land is not used as a park, then to Kenny and his heirs.

T	Stan to South Park in <u>fee simple</u>, but if the land is not used as a park, then to Kenny in <u>fee simple</u>
SoT	South Park - fee simple on executory limitation Kenny - shifting executory interest in fee simple

Kenny's interest violates RAP. The interests should read:

M(RAP)	South Park - fee simple

The words of purchase "to the City of South Park" denote South Park as the grantee of the present possessory interest; thus, the City receives the estate. The words of limitation "its successors and assigns" identify the estate as a fee simple. However, the words of limitation "but if" create a defeasible fee. Since the defeasible fee is followed by an interest in a third party, the City has a fee simple on executory limitation.

The words of purchase "to Kenny" denote Kenny as the grantee of a future interest. The words of limitation "and his heirs" identify the estate (that will exist if the future interest becomes possessory) as a fee simple. Since the defeasible fee is followed by an interest in a third party, Kenny's interest is an executory interest. It is a shifting interest because Kenny, a transferee, will divest the City, another transferee, of the estate.

2.   Note the contingent remainders, executory interests, and vested remainders subject to open

The Rule must be tested against Kenny's shifting executory interest. South Park's fee simple on executory limitation is a present possessory interest and therefore is deemed to be vested for purposes of the Rule.

3.   List the lives in being

Stan and Kenny are alive at the time of conveyance. Therefore, they are both lives in being. Remember, a life in being must be a real person. Thus, the City of South Park is not considered a life in being.

4.   Give birth to any potential afterborns

No children, issue, heirs, or widows are referred to in the conveyance. Kenny could have a son, Butters, in 2009.

5.   Kill the lives in being and add 21 years

Suppose that in 2010 Stan and Kenny both die in a common disaster. The lives in being are now dead. The "RAP line" becomes 2031.

6.   Is there any possibility of remote vesting (that a successor to Kenny's interest may gain possession past 2031)?

Is there any possibility that the executory interest may vest more than 21 years after all lives in being (Stan and Kenny) die (past the 2031 "RAP line")? If you said no, think more creatively. Imagine this possibility: 50 years after Stan and Kenny's deaths the City of South Park decides the land would make a much nicer parking garage than a park, and converts the land into this different use. According to the terms of the conveyance, the executory interest becomes possessory at that moment (likely, in a devisee or heir of Kenny who received the executory interest upon Kenny's death). The interest would vest in 2060, far beyond the 2031 "RAP line". RAP is violated. It is important to keep in mind that you are asking whether the future interest itself is capable of violating RAP; not whether the current holder of the interest will be alive when the interest vests. Again, the focus is on the interest and the conditions of its vesting; rather than on the identity of any current holders of the interest and whether they will vest in possession. The vesting of the executory interest is not dependent on Kenny being alive.

When a conveyance violates the Rule Against Perpetuities, it does so when it is made, not 21 years later. The interest is void ab initio, from the moment that it is created. In the absence of reform tools, the offending interest is struck. The conveyance now reads:

Stan ➔ City of South Park, its successors and assigns.

The City of South Park has a fee simple absolute.

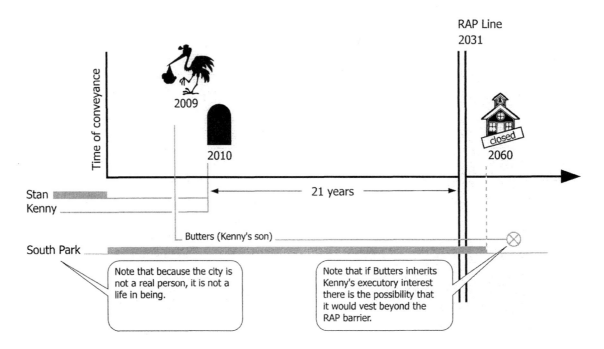

Modern Applications of RAP:

If the conveyance violates the traditional Rule, look at it one more time. Check to see if you are in a jurisdiction that: (i) looks to what actually happens during the perpetuities period applicable to the interest (Wait-and-See Doctrine); or (ii) permits reformation of the conveyance (Cy Pres Doctrine). If so, the conveyance may be saved.

Wait-and-See Jurisdiction: Wait until the end of the perpetuities period (lives in being plus 21 years). If at this point in time the interest has vested, it is good. However, if it has not yet vested, the interest fails. Using this approach, we would wait 21 years after the last of Stan or Kenney to die and see if the executory interest had vested. In this example, if the City continues to use the land for the stated purpose through the "RAP line," the executory interest would then (and only then, i.e., in 2031) be destroyed. If the land is converted to a different use sometime before the "RAP line", the executory interest vests.

Cy Pres Jurisdiction: The court can rewrite the conveyance consistent with the grantor's general intentions. If Cy Pres is utilized, the conveyance might read:

Stan ➔ the City of South Park, its successors and assigns, but if the land is not used as a park, then to Kenny and his heirs if Kenny is then alive.

Stan obviously wanted Kenny to benefit if the City did not keep the land as a park and, perhaps, trusted Kenny to respect his wishes with regard to the land. By changing the conveyance to include the requirement that Kenny be alive if the executory interest is to vest, a condition is created that prevents the future interest from vesting outside of the perpetuities period.

7.   Chef ➔ Kyle and his heirs so long as the house is not haunted; otherwise, to Kenny and his heirs.

T	
SoT	

M(RAP)	

7.   Chef ➜ Kyle and his heirs so long as the house is not haunted; otherwise, to Kenny and his heirs.

T	Chef to Kyle in <u>fee simple</u> so long as the house is not haunted; otherwise, to Kenny in <u>fee simple</u>	
SoT	Kyle Kenny	- fee simple on executory limitation - shifting executory interest in fee simple

Kenny's interest violates RAP. The interests should read:

M(RAP)	Kyle Chef	- fee simple determinable - possibility of reverter

The words of purchase "to Kyle" denote Kyle as the grantee of the present possessory interest; thus, he receives the estate. The words of limitation "and his heirs" identify the estate as a fee simple. The words of limitation "so long as" further identify the estate as a defeasible fee. Kyle's interest is defeasible because it will end automatically if the house becomes haunted (we will assume a house can be haunted). The words normally describe a fee simple determinable, but since they are followed by an interest in a third party, Kyle has a fee simple on executory limitation.

The words of purchase "to Kenny" denote Kenny as the grantee of a future interest. The words of limitation "and his heirs" identify the estate (that will exist if the future interest becomes possessory) as a fee simple. Since Kenny's future interest follows a defeasible fee, it is an executory interest. It is a shifting interest because Kenny, a transferee, will divest Kyle, another transferee, of the estate.

2.   Note the contingent remainders, executory interests, and vested remainders subject to open

The Rule must be tested against Kenny's shifting executory interest. Kyle's fee simple on executory limitation is a present possessory interest and therefore deemed to be vested for purposes of the Rule.

3.   List the lives in being

Chef, Kyle and Kenny are alive at the time of conveyance. Therefore, they are all lives in being.

4.   Give birth to any potential afterborns

No children, issue, heirs, or widows are referred to in the conveyance. In 2009, Kyle could have a son, Ike, and Kenny could have a son, Pip.

5.   Kill the lives in being and add 21 years

Suppose that in 2010 Chef, Kyle, and Kenny all die in tragic accident, seven days after watching the movie "The Ring". All lives in being are now dead. The "RAP line" becomes 2031.

6.   Is there any possibility of remote vesting (that the house will become haunted past 2031)?

Is there any possibility that the executory interest may vest more than 21 years after all lives in being (Chef, Kyle and Kenny) die (past the 2031 "RAP line")? One possibility: twenty-six years later, someone (born after the conveyance) sees a ghost (assuming such things are possible) in the upstairs hallway. Scientists confirm (and a court rules) that the house is haunted. The executory interest would then vest, a full five years after the death of Chef, Kyle and Kenny. Thus, the executory interest can vest more than 21 years after the death of the all lives in being. The interest violates RAP.

When a conveyance violates the Rule Against Perpetuities, it does so when it is made, not 21 years later. The interest is void ab initio, from the moment that it is created. In the absence of reform tools, the offending interest is struck. Hence, the executory interest held by Kenny is blue-penciled out.   The conveyance now reads:

Chef ➜ Kyle and his heirs so long as the house is not haunted.

Kyle has a fee simple determinable [determinable clauses are deemed to be part of the fee, and thus are not part of the blue-penciling]. Chef has a possibility of reverter (note, any future interest in the grantor is deemed to be vested in interest for purposes of the Rule).

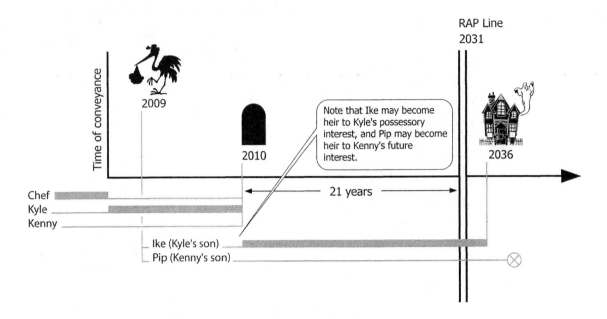

Modern Applications of RAP:

If the conveyance violates the traditional Rule, look at it one more time. Check to see if you are in a jurisdiction that: (i) looks to what actually happens during the perpetuities period applicable to the interest (Wait-and-See Doctrine); or (ii) permits reformation of the conveyance (Cy Pres Doctrine). If so, the conveyance may be saved.

Wait-and-See Jurisdiction: Wait until the end of the perpetuities period (lives in being plus 21 years). If at this point in time the interest has vested, it is good. However, if it has not yet vested, the interest fails. Using this approach, we would wait 21 years after Chef's, Kyle's and Kenny's death to see if the interest had vested. In this example, if the house does not become haunted within 21 years of the death of the lives in being, the interest is destroyed.

Cy Pres Jurisdiction: The court can rewrite the conveyance consistent with the grantor's intentions. If Cy Pres is utilized, the conveyance might read:

Chef ➔ Kyle and his heirs so long as the house is not haunted; otherwise, to Kenny and his heirs if Kenny is then alive.

The element of the conveyance that violates RAP is now avoided. Because the executory interest cannot possibly vest after Kenny dies, the conveyance does not violate the Rule. It will vest, if at all, during Kenny's life; it cannot vest remotely.

8.   Chef ➜ Kyle and his heirs so long the house is not haunted.

T	
SoT	

M(RAP)	

In a separate conveyance, Chef ➜ Kenny "all interest that I have."

T	
SoT	

M(RAP)	

8. Chef ➔ Kyle and his heirs so long the house is not haunted.

T	Chef to Kyle in <u>fee simple</u> so long the house is not haunted	
SoT	Kyle Chef	- fee simple determinable - possibility of reverter

M(RAP)	This conveyance is not subject to RAP.

In a separate conveyance, Chef ➔ Kenny "all interest that I have."

T	Chef to Kenny "all interest that I have"
SoT	Kenny - possibility of reverter

M(RAP)	This conveyance is not subject to RAP.

First conveyance: The words of purchase "to Kyle" denote Kyle as the grantee of the present possessory interest; thus, he receives the estate. The words of limitation "and his heirs" identify the estate as a fee simple. However, the words of limitation "so long as" create a fee simple determinable, which is a defeasible fee. The estate will automatically end if the house is ever haunted.

Chef retains a possibility of a reverter. Chef's interest automatically becomes possessory if the house becomes haunted.

Second conveyance: The words of purchase "to Kenny" denote Kenny as the grantee of Chef's interest. "All the interest Chef has" is a possibility of reverter. Kenny, therefore, gains Chef's possibility of reverter. Chef retains nothing.

2. Note the contingent remainder, executory interests, and vested remainders subject to open

There are no contingent remainders, executory interests, or vested remainders subject to open. Consequently, RAP does not apply.

Chef's conveyance to Kenny in a separate instrument did not create an executory interest, but rather passed on his possibility of reverter. Interests retained by the grantor are considered vested. Kenny's interest, therefore, is not subject to RAP. This is a common way of avoiding coming under the RAP umbrella.

9.   Kenny ➔ Stan for life, then to Stan's grandchildren for life, then to Kyle and his heirs.

   Facts: At the time of the conveyance, Stan had two children (Timmy and Phillip) and one grandchild (Ike).

T	
SoT	

M(RAP)	

9. Kenny ➔ Stan for life, then to Stan's grandchildren for life, then to Kyle and his heirs.

    Facts: At the time of the conveyance, Stan had two children (Timmy and Phillip) and one grandchild (Ike).

T	Kenny to Stan in <u>life estate</u>, then to Stan's grandchildren in <u>life estate</u>, then to Kyle in <u>fee simple</u>	
SoT	Stan	- life estate
	Stan's grandchild	- vested remainder in life estate subject to open
	Kyle	- vested remainder in fee simple

Stan's grandchild's interest violates RAP. The interests should read:

M(RAP)	Stan	- life estate
	Kyle	- vested remainder in fee simple

The words of purchase "to Stan" denote Stan as the grantee of the present possessory interest; thus, he receives the estate. The words of limitation "for life" identify the estate as a life estate.

The words of purchase "to Stan's grandchildren" denote the grantee(s) of a future interest. The words of limitation "for life" identify the estate (that will exist if the future interest becomes possessory) as a life estate. The interest is a remainder because (i) it is capable of becoming possessory immediately upon expiration of the preceding estate and (ii) it cannot divest any other interests. It is vested because (i) a grandchild of Stan's is ascertainable at the time of the conveyance and (ii) there are no conditions precedent. The vested remainder of Stan's grandchild is subject to open (sometimes called subject to divestment) because more grandchildren may be born to Stan after the creation of the interest.

The words of purchase "to Kyle" denote Kyle as the grantee of a future interest. The words of limitation "and his heirs" identify the estate (that will exist if the future interest becomes possessory) as a fee simple. Kyle's interest is a remainder because (i) it is capable of becoming possessory immediately upon the expiration of the preceding estate and (ii) it cannot divest any other interests. It is vested because (i) Kyle is ascertainable at the time of the conveyance and (ii) there is no condition precedent.

2. Note the contingent remainders, executory interests, and vested remainders subject to open

The Rule must be tested against the vested remainder subject to open. Stan's life estate and Kyle's vested remainder (respectively, a present possessory interest and a vested future interest) are vested for purposes of the Rule.

3. List the lives in being

Kenny, Stan, Kyle, Timmy, Phillip and Ike are all alive at the time of conveyance. Therefore, they are all lives in being.

4. Give birth to any potential afterborns

Stan, Timmy, and/or Phillip could have additional children after the conveyance. If Stan has another child AFTER the conveyance, that child is NOT a life in being for purposes of the Rule (since that child was not alive at the time of the conveyance). The same holds for Timmy and/or Phillip. Note, even if Stan was of an age considered to be beyond fertility, at common law he is still considered capable of conceiving a child; he also could adopt.

Suppose that in early 2009, Stan has another child, Cartman (not a life in being at the time of the creation of the remainder). Imagine that Cartman has a child, Stinky, twenty-six years later (Stinky would be Stan's grandchild, and not a life in being at the time of the creation of the remainder).

5. Kill the lives in being and add 21 years

Suppose that in late 2010, Kenny, Stan, Kyle, Timmy, Phillip and Ike all die in a flood. All lives in being are now dead. The "RAP line" becomes 2031.

6. Is there any possibility of remote vesting (that a grandchild's interest may vest past 2031)?

Is there any possibility that the vested remainder subject to open may vest more than 21 years after all lives in being (Kenny, Stan, Kyle, Timmy, Phillip and Ike) die (past the 2031 "RAP line")? One possibility: Stan has another child, Cartman (not a life in being), in early 2009. In late 2010, Kenny, Stan, Kyle, Timmy, Phillip and Ike all die in a common disaster. Cartman (not a life in being) can have Stinky (not a life in being) in 2035. Stinky's interest would vest at birth (in 2035), which is far beyond the 2031 "RAP line".

Because additional children of Stan may be born after the conveyance (and thus not be lives in being),who can have children who are not lives in being, RAP is violated – these grandchildren's interests will vest only at their birth sometime in the future, which might be well past the "RAP line". Remember, only one example of remote vesting need be shown; that there may be many instances of vesting within the "RAP line" is of no consequence.

Note, in this problem, Kyle's future interest is a vested remainder in fee simple, and, therefore, is not subject to RAP.

When a conveyance violates the Rule Against Perpetuities, it does so when it is made, not 21 years later. The interest is void ab initio, from the moment that it is created. In the absence of reform tools, the offending interest is struck. The conveyance now reads:

Kenny ➔ Stan for life, then to Kyle and his heirs

Stan has a life estate and Kyle as a vested remainder in fee simple.

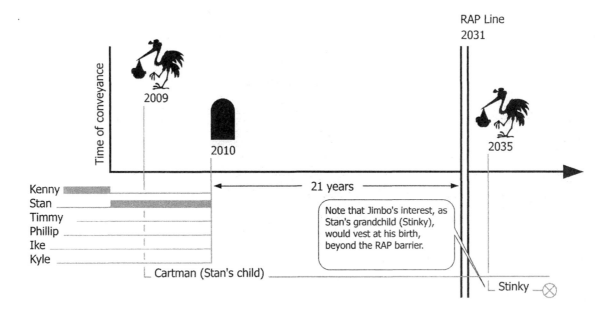

Modern Applications:

If the conveyance violates the traditional Rule, look at it one more time. Check to see if you are in a jurisdiction that: (i) looks to what actually happens during the perpetuities period applicable to the interest (Wait-and-See Doctrine); or (ii) permits reformation of the conveyance (Cy Pres Doctrine). If so, the conveyance may be saved.

Wait-and-See Jurisdiction: Wait until the end of the perpetuities period (lives in being plus 21 years). If at this point in time the interest has vested, it is good. However, if it has not yet vested, the interest fails. Using this approach, we would wait 21 years after the death of all lives in being to see if the interest had vested. In this example, we would see if Stan had any more children after the conveyance was written, and if he did, we would have to see if those children had any children of their own within the "RAP line". The class of grandchildren would be closed in 2031; all grandchildren (born by that date) gain a vested interest. None born thereafter would have any interest.

Cy Pres Jurisdiction: The court can rewrite the conveyance consistent with the grantor's intentions. If Cy Pres is utilized, the conveyance might read:

Kenny ➔ Stan for life, then to Stan's grandchildren [by Timmy and Phillip] for life, then to Kyle and his heirs

Since Timmy and Phillip are lives in being, we are certain that all of their children will be born, at the latest, by the last one of Timmy and Phillip to die. Therefore, there is no possibility of remote vesting.

10.   Kenny ➜ Chef for life, then to Chef's widow for life, then to Chef's children then living.

Facts: At the time of the conveyance, Chef is married to The Mayor and has no children.

T	
SoT	

M(RAP)	

10.   Kenny ➔ Chef for life, then to Chef's widow for life, then to Chef's children then living.

Facts: At the time of the conveyance, Chef is married to The Mayor and has no children.

T	Kenny to Chef in <u>life estate</u>, then to Chef's widow in <u>life estate</u>, then to Chef's children then living in <u>fee simple</u>
SoT	Chef - life estate Chef's widow - contingent remainder in life estate Chef's children then living - contingent remainder in fee simple Kenny - reversion

Chef's first child's interest violates RAP. The interests should read:

M(RAP)	Chef - life estate Chef's widow - contingent remainder in life estate Kenny - reversion

The words of purchase "to Chef" denote Chef as the grantee of the present possessory interest; thus, he receives the estate. The words of limitation "for life" identify the estate as a life estate.

The words of purchase "to Chef's widow" denote Chef's widow as the grantee of a future interest. The words of limitation "for life" identify the estate (that will exist if the future interest becomes possessory) as a life estate. The interest is a remainder because (i) it is capable of becoming possessory immediately upon the expiration of the preceding estate and (ii) it cannot divest any other interests. It is a contingent remainder because Chef's widow is not ascertainable until Chef dies. (The Mayor may die before Chef or Chef may get a divorce and then remarry.)

The words of purchase "to Chef's children then living" denote Chef's children living at the time of the widow's death as the grantee(s) of a future interest. There are no words of limitation, so a fee simple is presumed. The interest is a remainder because (i) it is capable of becoming possessory immediately upon the expiration of the preceding estate and (ii) it cannot divest any other interests. It is a contingent remainder both because, at the time of the conveyance, Chef's children then living are not ascertainable (you cannot point to them; they can only be identified at the widow's death). Chef's children who are alive at his widow's death will receive the estate at the end of Chef's widow's life estate - if they have been born and are still alive.

Kenny retains a future interest known as a reversion. A reversion will always follow a contingent remainder since someone must hold seisin in the estate at all times. Since a contingent remainder is not certain to vest, the grantor must retain a reversion. Kenny's reversion will vest in the event Chef dies without a child who is alive at his widow's death.

2.   Note the contingent remainders, executory interests, and vested remainders subject to open

The Rule must be tested against the two contingent remainders of Chef's widow and Chef's children. Chef's life estate and Kenny's reversion (respectively, a present possessory interest and a future interest in the grantor) are deemed to be vested for purposes of the Rule.

3.   List the lives in being

Kenny, Chef, and The Mayor are alive at the time of conveyance. Therefore, they are all lives in being.

4.   Give birth to any potential afterborns

Even if Chef is happily married to The Mayor, they could divorce or she might die before him. Chef could remarry an individual who was not yet born at the time of the grant (Tina). Chef could also have a child (Ike) sometime after the conveyance, either with The Mayor or with Tina. Neither Tina nor Ike is a life in being for the purposes of the Rule, since neither was alive at the time of the conveyance.

5. Kill the lives in being and add 21 years

Suppose that Chef, Kenney and The Mayor are killed by a volcanic eruption in 2030. All lives in being are now dead. The "RAP line" becomes 2051.

6. Is there any possibility of remote vesting [that (i) Chef's widow will be only ascertained, or (ii) a child of Chef may be alive -- past 2051]?

(i) Is there any possibility that the contingent remainder in Chef's widow may vest more than 21 years after the last life in being (Kenny, Chef and The Mayor) die (past 2051)? No. The widow's interest is certain to vest, if at all, upon Chef's death (in 2030). Even though Chef's widow may not be a life in being at the time of the conveyance, she must be his wife, at latest, by the date of his death. The moment Chef dies, his widow is ascertainable (if he is married), and her interest vests. If Chef was not married when he died, the contingent interest vanishes. Either way, the widow's interest will certainly either vest or not when Chef, a life in being, dies. There is no possibility of remote vesting; therefore, the contingent remainder in the widow is a valid interest under the Rule.

(ii) Is there any possibility that the contingent remainder in Chef's children may vest more than 21 years after the last life in being (Kenny, Chef and The Mayor) dies (past 2051)? One possibility: Suppose that in 2009 Chef divorces The Mayor. Tina is born the same day. Twenty years later, Chef and Tina marry. Ike is born in early 2030. Thus, as of early 2030, Chef is married to Tina (not a life in being at creation of the interest) and has a child Ike (not a life in being at creation of the interest). Celebrating Ike's birth, Kenny, Chef and The Mayor die when their cigars mysteriously explode. The lives in being are now dead, and the 21 year period begins (and lasts until 2051).

Tina, Chef's widow, now has a life estate. The interest in Chef's first child, Ike, cannot vest until Tina dies (the contingent remainder vests only at the death of the widow; "children then living" = children living at the widow's death). If Tina and Ike live more than 21 years past Chef's death, RAP will be violated. If Tina dies in 2060 and Ike is still alive at his mother's death, then Ike becomes a "child then living" and the contingent remainder vests. RAP is violated.

When a conveyance violates the Rule Against Perpetuities, it does so when it is made, not 21 years later. The interest is void ab initio, from the moment that it is created. In the absence of reform tools, the offending interest is struck. The conveyance now reads:

Kenny ➔ Chef for life, then to Chef's widow for life.

Chef has a life estate, Chef's widow has a contingent remainder in life estate, and Kenny retains a reversion.

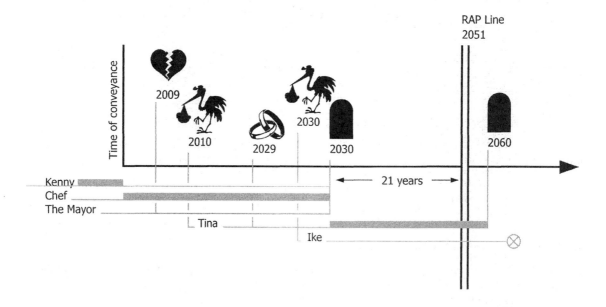

Modern Applications:

If the conveyance violates the traditional Rule, look at it one more time. Check to see if you are in a jurisdiction that: (i) looks to what actually happens during the perpetuities period applicable to the interest (Wait-and-See Doctrine); or (ii) permits reformation of the conveyance (Cy Pres Doctrine). If so, the conveyance may be saved.

Wait-and-See Jurisdiction: Wait until the end of the perpetuities period (lives in being plus 21 years). If at this point in time the interest has vested, it is good. However, if it has not yet vested, the interest fails. Using this approach, we would wait until 21 years after the last of Kenny, Chef, or The Mayor to die, and see if the interest has vested. In this example, if Chef's widow dies within 21 years after the last of Kenny, Chef, or The Mayor to die, and a child of Chef is living at the widow's death, that child will receive the estate.

Cy Pres Jurisdiction: The court can rewrite the conveyance consistent with the grantor's intentions. If Cy Pres is utilized, the conveyance might read:

Kenny ➔ Chef for life, then to Chef's widow for life, then to Chef's children who are alive at the death of Chef's widow and who are now living.

By adding the phrase "now living," the children become lives in being at the creation of the interest and therefore make remote vesting impossible.

V. Review Problems

A mixed set of review problems follows. For each conveyance, supply the correct state of title, identify any applicable rules furthering marketability, and provide a complete analysis.

Remember, proceed slowly and deliberately through your analysis. First translate all words of limitation; then apply the rules you have learnt.

If you have worked diligently through the earlier parts of this Workbook, these problems should provide comforting evidence of your mastery of the material.

1. Aadi ➜ Kael for life, then to Kael's children and their heirs.

    Fact: Kael has two children, Tom and Jerry.

T	
SoT	

2. Tab ➜ Jacinthe and her heirs, but if Jacinthe gets married, then to Eddy and the heirs of his body.

T	
SoT	

1.   Aadi ➔ Kael for life, then to Kael's children and their heirs.

Fact: Kael has two children, Tom and Jerry.

T	Aadi to Kael in <u>life estate</u>, then to Kael's children in <u>fee simple</u>	
SoT	Kael Kael's children	- life estate - vested remainder in fee simple subject to open

The words of purchase "to Kael" denote Kael as the grantee of the present possessory interest, thus he receives the estate. The words of limitation "for life" describe the estate as a life estate.

The words of purchase "to Kael's children" denote Kael's children as the grantees of the future interest. The words of limitation "and their heirs" describe the interest (that will exist if the future interest becomes possessory) as a fee simple. The interest is a remainder because (i) it is capable of becoming possessory immediately upon the expiration of the preceding estate and (ii) it cannot divest any other interest. It is vested because (i) Tom and Jerry are ascertainable at the time of the conveyance [you can point to them] and (ii) there is no condition precedent. It is subject to open because Kael may have more children.

2.   Tab ➔ Jacinthe and her heirs, but if Jacinthe gets married, then to Eddy and the heirs of his body.

T	Tab to Jacinthe in <u>fee simple</u>, but if Jacinthe gets married, then to Eddy in <u>fee tail</u>	
SoT	Jacinthe Eddy Tab	- fee simple on executory limitation - shifting executory interest in fee tail - reversion

The words of purchase "to Jacinthe" denote Jacinthe as the grantee of the present possessory interest, thus she receives the estate. The words of limitation "and her heirs" describe the estate as fee simple. The words "but if" are words of limitation that create a defeasible fee. Since the defeasible fee is followed by an interest in a third party, Jacinthe holds the estate on executory limitation. If Jacinthe marries she will lose the estate.

The words of purchase "to Eddy" denote Eddy as the grantee of a future interest. The words of limitation "and the heirs of his body" describe the interest (that will exist if the future interest becomes possessory) as a fee tail [in those jurisdictions recognizing the estate]. Since this is a future interest in a third party which follows a defeasible fee, the interest is an executory interest. It is a shifting executory interest because Eddy, a transferee, divests Jacinthe, another transferee. Eddy's interest will become possessory if Jacinthe marries.

Since Tab carved out a potentially smaller estate from his larger fee simple, he retains a future interest known as a reversion. Tab's reversion becomes possessory if, and when, Jacinthe gets married and the direct line Eddy's of descendants ends.

The executory interest does not violate the Rule Against Perpetuities. Jacintheis a life in being at the creation of the interest. We know for certain that the condition (Jacinthe gets married) will happen, if at all, during a life in being's lifetime (Jacinthe's). There is no possibility of remote vesting.

3.	Gerard ➔ Brand for life, then to Benedict for life if Benedict conquers Sparta, then to Dara and her heirs.

T	
SoT	

3.   Gerard ➜ Brand for life, then to Benedict for life if Benedict conquers Sparta, then to Dara and her heirs.

T	Gerard to Brand in <u>life estate</u>, then to Benedict in <u>life estate</u> if Benedict conquers Sparta, then to Dara in <u>fee simple</u>.
SoT	Brand - life estate Benedict - contingent remainder in life estate Dara - vested remainder in fee simple

The words of purchase "to Brand" denote Brand as the grantee of the present possessory interest; thus, he receives the estate. The words of limitation "for life" identify the estate as a life estate.

The words of purchase "to Benedict" denote Benedict as the grantee of a future interest. The words of limitation "for life" identify the estate (that will exist if the future interest becomes possessory) as a life estate. The interest is a remainder because (i) it is capable of becoming possessory immediately upon the expiration of the preceding estate and (ii) it cannot divest any other interests. It is a contingent remainder because it is subject to the condition precedent that Benedict conquers Sparta.

The words of purchase "to Dara" denote Dara as the grantee of a future interest. The words of limitation "and his heirs" identify the estate (that will exist if the future interest becomes possessory) as a fee simple. The interest is a remainder because (i) it is capable of becoming possessory immediately upon the expiration of the preceding estate and (ii) it cannot divest any other interests. It is vested because (i) Dara is ascertainable at the time of the conveyance [you can point to her] and (ii) there is no condition precedent.

The contingent remainder does not violate the Rule Against Perpetuities. Benedict is a life in being at the creation of the interest. We know for certain that the condition (Benedict conquers Sparta) will happen, if at all, during a life in being's lifetime (Benefict's). There is no possibility of remote vesting.

4.   Iago ➔ Rafael for life, then to Rafael's heirs for life.

T	
SoT	

4.   Iago ➜ Rafael for life, then to Rafael's heirs for life.

T	Iago to Rafael in <u>life estate</u>, then to Rafael's heirs in <u>life estate</u>.
SoT	Rafael - life estate Rafael's heirs - contingent remainder in life estate Iago - reversion

The rule in Shelley's Case applies. The interests should read:

M(SC)	Rafael - life estate Iago - reversion

The words of purchase "to Rafael" denote Rafael as the grantee of the present possessory interest; thus, he receives the estate. The words of limitation "for life" identify the estate as a life estate.

The words of purchase "to Rafael's heirs" denote the grantee(s) of a future interest. The words of limitation "for life" identify the estate (that will exist if the future interest becomes possessory) as a life estate. The interest is a remainder because (i) it is capable of becoming possessory immediately upon the expiration of the preceding estate and (ii) it cannot divest any other interests. It is contingent because, at the time of the conveyance, Rafael's heirs are unascertainable [you cannot point to them].

Iago retains a future interest known as a reversion. A reversion will always follow a contingent remainder because someone must hold seisin in the estate at all times. Since a contingent remainder is not certain to vest, the grantor must retain a reversion.

Shelley's Rule applies because there is one instrument creating a life estate in a transferee (Rafael), followed by a remainder in that transferee's (Rafael's) heirs, and both the life estate and the remainder are legal interests. The remainder in Rafael's heirs becomes a remainder in fee simple in Rafael. In effect, the words of purchase [Rafael's heirs] become words of limitation [Rafael and heirs]. It is vested because (i) Rafael is ascertainable [you can point to him] and (ii) there is no condition precedent.

Rafael's vested remainder in life estate does not give him anything more than his initial present possessory life estate. When Rafeal dies, he loses all interest in the property. Economy suggests that Rafael be characterized as having simply a life estate. Iago's reversion stands ready to become possessory upon Rafael's death.

5. Mabel ➜ Dahlia for life, then to Dahlia's heirs.

    Fact: This jurisdiction that does not apply the Rule in Shelley's Case, but does apply the Doctrine of Destructibility of Contingent Remainders

T	
SoT	

5.   Mabel ➜ Dahlia for life, then to Dahlia's heirs.

Fact: This jurisdiction that does not apply the Rule in Shelley's Case, but does apply the Doctrine of Destructibility of Contingent Remainders

T	Mabel to Dahlia in <u>life estate</u>, then to Dahlia's heirs in <u>fee simple</u>.	
SoT	Dahlia Dahlia's heirs Mabel	- life estate - contingent remainder in fee simple - reversion

The words of purchase "to Dahlia" denote Dahlia as the grantee of the present possessory interest; thus, she receives the estate. The words of limitation "for life" identify the estate as a life estate.

The words of purchase "to Dahlia's heirs" denote Dahlia's heirs as the grantee(s) of a future interest. There are no words of limitation, so a fee simple is presumed. The interest is a remainder because (i) it is capable of becoming possessory immediately upon the expiration of the preceding estate and (ii) it cannot divest any other interests. It is contingent because, at the time of the conveyance, Dahlia's heirs are unascertainable [you cannot point to them].

Mabel retains a future interest known as a reversion. A reversion will always follow a contingent remainder because someone must hold seisin in the estate at all times. Since contingent remainders are not certain to vest, the grantor must retain a reversion.

Although the elements for Shelley's Case are present, this jurisdiction does not apply Shelley's Case to conveyances. In a destructibility jurisdiction, a contingent remainder that is not ready to vest at the termination of the preceding estate is destroyed. Here, it is certain that the contingent remainder in Dahlia's heirs will vest, if at all, immediately upon Dahlia's death. She either has heirs at her death, or not; there is no way for her to have heirs that are established sometime in the future after the moment of death. If we "wait and see," nothing will change. Therefore, the contingent remainder is not destructible. [The result would be the same in a non-destructibility jurisdiction.]

6.   Fiona ➔ Corwin for as long as Corwin lives.

T	
SoT	

6.   Fiona ➜ Corwin for as long as Corwin lives.

T	Fiona to Corwin in <u>life estate</u>.	
SoT	Corwin	- life estate
	Fiona	- reversion

The words of purchase "to Corwin" denote Corwin as the grantee of the present possessory interest; thus, he receives the estate. There are no traditional words of limitation present in the conveyance; however, the words "for as long as Corwin lives" identify the grantor's intent to create a life estate. Thus, Corwin receives a life estate.

Since Fiona carved out a smaller estate from her larger fee simple, she retains a future interest known as a reversion, which will become possessory upon the expiration of the life estate.

7.   Joachim ➜ Ernestine and his heirs provided that the family home is not built in Meinz, and if it is Joachim shall have the right to re-enter and retake the estate.

T	
SoT	

7.   Joachim ➜   Ernestine and his heirs provided that the family home is not built in Meinz,
            and if it is Joachim shall have the right to re-enter and retake the estate.

T	Joachim to Ernestine in <u>fee simple</u> **provided that** (subject to a condition subsequent) the family home is not built in Meinz.
SoT	Ernestine - fee simple subject to a condition subsequent Joachim - right of entry

The words of purchase "to Ernestine" denote Ernestine as the grantee of the present possessory interest; thus, he receives the estate. The words of limitation "and his heirs" identify the estate as a fee simple. However, the words of limitation "provided that" create a fee simple subject to a condition subsequent, which is a defeasible fee. The conveyance also includes express words of re-entry which further describe the defeasible fee as a fee simple subject to a condition subsequent. The estate can be cut short if the express condition is broken. Ernestine has a fee simple subject to a condition subsequent. He (or his grantee, devisee, or heir) can lose the estate if the family home is built in Meinz and Joachim (or his grantee, devisee, or heir) reenter and reclaim the estate.

Joachim, the grantor, retains a future interest known as a right of entry (power of termination). Upon the happening of the stated event, the grantor has the right to re-enter the estate (unlike the fee simple determinable, the estate will not automatically end). The grantor must take affirmative action and exercise this right to regain possession of the estate.

8.   Ulf ➜ My first relative to discover a new plant species and his heirs.

T	
SoT	

8. Ulf ➔ My first relative to discover a new plant species and his heirs.

T	Ulf to my first relative to discover a new plant species in <u>fee simple</u>.
SoT	Ulf - fee simple on executory limitation 1st relative… - springing executory interest in fee simple

RAP has been violated. There is no valid conveyance.

M(RAP)	Ulf retains a fee simple.

The words of purchase "to my first relative to discover a new plant species" denote the grantee of an estate. The words of limitation "and his heirs" identify the estate as a fee simple. However, the conveyance states a condition which must occur prior to the relative gaining possession; therefore, the relative's interest is a future interest. Because the future interest will divest the grantor of the estate, the interest is an executory interest. It is a springing executory interest because the relative, a transferee, will divest Ulf, the transferor, of the estate.

Ulf has present possession of the estate. He holds a fee simple on executory limitation (subject to divestment). His interest will be cut short if one of his relatives discovers a new plant species.

Because the conveyance created an executory interest, one must consider whether or not the interest violates RAP:

List the lives in being:

Ulf and all relatives living at the time of conveyance (assume they are Xi and Fae) are the all lives in being.

Give birth to any potential afterborns:

Xi could have a son, Yao, after the conveyance. Yao is not a life in being for purposes of the Rule.

Kill off the lives in being and add 21 years:

Suppose that in late 2010 Ulf, Xi and Fae all die of malaria in Brasil while hunting for a new species of orchid. The lives in being are now dead. The "RAP line" becomes 2031.

Is there any possibility of remote vesting (that a relative not born at the time of the conveyance could discover a new plant species after 2031)?

Is there any possibility that the executory interest may vest more than 21 years after all lives in being (Ulf, Xi and Fae) die (past the 2031 "RAP line")? One possibility: Yao is born in early 2010 (and therefore is not a life in being at creation). Yao visits Brasil in 2050 and discovers a new species of teal orchid. The executory interest vests in 2050; RAP is violated. In the absence of reform tools, the offending interest is struck. In this case, there would be no conveyance. The executory interest is void.

However, if you are in a jurisdiction that (i) looks to what actually happens during the perpetuities period; or (ii) permits the reformation of the conveyance (Cy Pres), then the conveyance may be saved.

Wait and See Jurisdiction: Wait until the end of the perpetuities period (lives in being plus 21 years). If at this point in time the interest has vested, it is good. However, if it has not yet vested, the interest fails. Using this approach, we would wait 21 years after the last of Ulf, Xi and Fae to die and see if any relative's interest had vested. In this example, if a relative of Ulf's discovered a new species of plant within 21 years of the last of them to die, she would take the estate in fee simple absolute.

Cy Pres Jurisdiction: The court can rewrite the conveyance consistent with the grantor's general intentions. If Cy Pres is utilized, the conveyance might read:

Ulf ➔ My first relative who is now living to discover a new plant species

9.   Dobb ➜   Gunther and his heirs, but if Elizabeth cashes out the trust fund, then to Dobb who may
            enter and terminate the estate.

T	
SoT	

9.   Dobb ➔ Gunther and his heirs, but if Elizabeth cashes out the trust fund, then to Dobb who may enter and terminate the estate.

T	Dobb to Gunther in <u>fee simple</u>, but if Elizabeth cashes out the trust fund, then to Dobb in <u>fee simple</u>.	
SoT	Gunther	- fee simple subject to a condition subsequent
	Dobb	- right of entry

The words of purchase "to Gunther" denote Gunther as the grantee of the present possessory interest; thus, he receives the estate. The words of limitation "and his heirs" identify the estate as a fee simple. However, the words "but if" are words of limitation that create a fee simple subject to condition subsequent, which is a defeasible fee. The estate can be cut short if Elizabeth ever cashes out the trust fund.

Dobb, the grantor, retrains a future interest known as a right of entry (power of termination). Upon the happening of the stated event, the grantor has the right to re-enter the estate. The grantor must take affirmative action and exercise this right to regain possession of the estate. The estate of the grantee continues until the grantor exercises the right of entry. If Elizabeth cashes out the trust fund, Dobb (or his grantee, devisee, or heir) has the right to re-enter and reclaim the estate.

10.   Jabir ➜ Esther for life, then to Jabir's heirs.

T	
SoT	

10.   Jabir ➜ Esther for life, then to Jabir's heirs.

T	Jabir to Esther in <u>life estate</u>, then to Jabir's heirs in <u>fee simple</u>.	
SoT	Esther Jabir's heir's Jabir	- life estate - contingent remainder in fee simple - reversion

Doctrine of Worthier Title applies. The interests should read:

M(WT)	Esther Jabir	- life estate - reversion

The words of purchase "to Esther" denote Esther as the grantee of the present possessory interest; thus, she receives the estate. The words of limitation "for life" identify the estate as a life estate.

The words of purchase "to Jabir's heirs" denote the grantee(s) of a future interest. There are no words of limitation, so a fee simple is presumed. The interest is a remainder because (i) it is capable of becoming possessory immediately upon the expiration of the preceding estate and (ii) it cannot divest any other interests. It is a contingent remainder because, at the time of the conveyance, Jabir's heirs are unascertainable [you cannot point to them].

Jabir retains a future interest known as a reversion. A reversion will always follow a contingent remainder because someone must hold seisin in the estate at all times. Since a contingent remainder is not certain to vest, the grantor must retain a reversion.

The Doctrine of Worthier Title applies because the conveyance is inter vivos, and a future interest (a remainder) was created in the grantor's (Jabir's) heirs. Under the rule, the presumption is that no interest is created in Jabir's heirs; rather Jabir (the grantor) intends to retain a future interest in himself. In effect, the words of purchase ("to Jabir's heirs") become words of limitation ("to Jabir and heirs). Jabir has given away only a life estate; he retains all other interests in himself. He has a reversion.

11.   Jasper ➔ Onyx and the heirs of her body.

T	
SoT	

11.   Jasper ➔ Onyx and the heirs of her body.

T	Jasper to Onyx in <u>fee tail</u>.
SoT	Onyx - fee tail Jasper - reversion

The words of purchase "to Onyx" denote Onyx as the grantee of the present possessory interest; thus, he receives the estate. The words of limitation "and the heirs of her body" identify the estate as a fee tail, in those jurisdictions recognizing the estate.

Since Jasper carved out a smaller estate from his larger fee simple, he retains a future interest known as a reversion. Jasper's interest will become possessory if the issue line of Onyx ceases.

12.   Bleys ➔ Oberon for life, then to Oberon's widow and her heirs, but if she remarries, to Caine and his heirs.

Fact: Oberon is unmarried.

T	
SoT	

12.   Bleys ➜ Oberon for life, then to Oberon's widow and her heirs, but if she remarries, to Caine and his heirs.

Fact: Oberon is unmarried.

T	Bleys to Oberon in <u>life estate</u>, then to Oberon's widow in <u>fee simple</u>, but if she remarries, to Caine in <u>fee simple</u>.	
SoT	Oberon	- life estate
	Oberon's widow	- contingent remainder in fee simple on executory limitation
	Caine	- shifting executory interest in fee simple
	Bleys	- reversion

Caine's interest violates RAP. The interests should read:

M(RAP)	Oberon	- life estate
	Oberon's widow	- contingent remainder in fee simple
	Bleys	- reversion

The words of purchase "to Oberon" denote Oberon as the grantee of the present possessory interest; thus, he receives the estate. The words of limitation "for life" identify the estate as a life estate.

The words of purchase "to Oberon's widow" denote Oberon's widow as the grantee of a future interest. The words of limitation "and her heirs" identify the estate (that will exist if the future interest becomes possessory) as a fee simple. The interest is a remainder because (i) it is capable of becoming possessory immediately upon the expiration of the preceding estate and (ii) it cannot divest any other interests. It is contingent because Oberon's widow is not ascertainable until Oberon dies [you cannot point to her]. The words "but if" are words of limitation that create a defeasible fee. Since Oberon's widow's defeasible fee is followed by a future interest in a third party, Oberon's widow has a contingent remainder in fee simple on executory limitation. Her estate may end if she remarries.

The words of purchase "to Caine" denote Caine as the grantee of a future interest. The words of limitation "and his heirs" identify the estate (that will exist if the future interest becomes possessory) as a fee simple. Since Caine's estate follows a defeasible fee in fee simple, it is an executory interest. Caine will gain possession of the estate only if Oberon's widow remarries. If she does not remarry, Caine's interest cannot vest and will be destroyed when Oberon's widow dies. It is a shifting interest because Caine, a transferee, will divest Oberon's widow, another transferee, of the estate.

Note, the "but if" does not create alternative contingent remainders. Here, the widow's interest can vest and Caine's interest can vest. With alternative contingent remainders, if one vests, the other cannot.

Because the conveyance creates a contingent remainder and an executory interest, one must consider whether or not the interests violate RAP:

List the lives in being:

Bley, Oberon and Caine are the all lives in being.

Give birth to any potential afterborns:

Suppose Sue and Henry are born one year after the conveyance. They are not lives in being for purposes of the Rule.

Kill off the lives in being and add 21 years:

Suppose that in 2040, Bley, Oberon and Caine all die in a common disaster. The lives in being are now dead. The "RAP line" becomes 2061 (2040 + 21).

Is there any possibility of remote vesting [that (i) the widow will be only ascertained or (ii) the widow remarries –past 2061]?

(i) Is there any possibility that the contingent remainder in Oberon's widow may vest more than 21 years after the last life in being (Bley, Oberon and Caine) dies (past 2061)? No. The widow's interest is certain to vest, if at all, upon Oberon's death (in 2040). Even though Oberon's widow may not be a life in being at the time of the conveyance, she must be his wife, at latest, by the date of his death. The moment Oberon dies, his widow is ascertainable (if he is married) and her interest vests. There is no possibility of remote vesting; therefore, the contingent remainder in the widow is a valid interest under the Rule.

(ii) Is there any possibility that the executory interest in Caine may vest more than 21 years after the last life in being (Bley, Oberon and Caine) dies (past 2061)? One possibility: Suppose that Sue is born one year after the conveyance. In 2030, Oberon marries Sue (who was not alive at the time of the conveyance). When Caine dies in 2040, Sue is Oberon's widow. In 2065, Sue marries Henry (who also was not alive at the time of the conveyance). RAP is violated.

In the absence of reform tools, the offending interest is struck. The conveyance now reads:

Bleys ➔ Oberon for life, then to Oberon's widow and his heirs.

Oberon has a life estate, and Oberon's widow has a contingent remainder in fee simple. Bleys retains a reversion. Caine gets nothing.

Wait-and-See Jurisdiction: We would wait 21 years after the death of all lives in being to see if the interest has vested. In this example, if Oberon's widow remarries within that time, then Caine's interest would vest. If the widow did not remarry, then Caine's interest would be struck.

Cy Pres Jurisdiction: The court can rewrite the conveyance consistent with the grantor's general intentions. Utilizing Cy Pres, the conveyance might read:

Bleys ➔ Oberon for life, then to Oberon's widow and her heirs, but if she remarries, to Caine and his heirs if Caine is then alive.

13. Albert ➜ Cameron and his heirs, but if Christina is unfaithful, then Albert may enter and terminate the estate.

T	
SoT	

13. Albert ➔ Cameron and his heirs, but if Christina is unfaithful, then Albert may enter and terminate the estate.

T	Albert to Cameron in <u>fee simple</u>, but if Christina is unfaithful, then to Albert in <u>fee simple</u>.
SoT	Cameron — fee simple subject to a condition subsequent Albert — right of entry

The words of purchase "to Cameron" denote Cameron as the grantee of the present possessory interest; thus, he receives the estate. The words of limitation "and his heirs" identify the estate as a fee simple. However, the words "but if" are words of limitation that create a fee simple subject to condition subsequent, which is a defeasible fee. The estate can be cut short if Christina ever is unfaithful.

Albert, the grantor, retrains a future interest known as a right of entry (power of termination). Upon the happening of the stated event, the grantor has the right to re-enter and reclaim the estate. The grantor must take affirmative action and exercise this right to regain possession of the estate. The estate of the grantee continues until the grantor exercises the right of entry. If Christina is unfaithful, Albert (or his grantee, devisee, or heir) has the right to re-enter and reclaim the estate.

14.   Bonta ➔ Makoto until the death of Koizumi.

T	
SoT	

14.   Bonta ➔ Makoto until the death of Koizumi.

T	Bonta to Makoto in <u>life estate</u>	
SoT	Makoto Bonta	- life estate per autre vie - reversion

The words of purchase "to Makoto" denote Makoto as the grantee of the present possessory interest; thus, she receives the estate. The words of limitation "until the death of Koizumi" identify the estate as a life estate per autre vie (for the life of another). Makoto has a life estate measured by the length of Koizumi's life.

Since Bonta carved out a smaller estate from his larger estate, he retains a future interest known as a reversion which will become possessory upon the end of the life estate. Bonta (or his grantee, devisee, or heir) will gain possession of the estate at the death of Koizumi.

If Koizumi dies before Makoto, the life estate expires, and Bonta's reversion becomes possessory. However, if Makoto dies before Koizumi, the estate passes either by Makoto's will or by intestate succession to her heirs. Her devisees or heirs only have an interest in the estate until the death of Koizumi.

Koizumi gains no interest in the estate; he serves only as the measuring life for the conveyance.

15.   Obelix ➔ Asterix for ten years, but if Asterix leaves the Gaelic resistance during that time, then to Idefix and his heirs.

T	
SoT	

15.   Obelix ➔ Asterix for ten years, but if Asterix leaves the Gaelic resistance during that time, then to Idefix and his heirs.

T	Obelix to Asterix for <u>a term of years</u>, but if Asterix leaves the Gaelic resistance during that time, then to Idefix in <u>fee simple</u>	
SoT	Asterix	- term of years on executory limitation
	Idefix	- shifting executory interest in fee simple
	Obelix	- reversion

The words of purchase "to Asterix" denote Asterix as the grantee of the present possessory interest; thus, he receives the estate. The words of limitation "for ten years" create a term of years, which is an estate of fixed duration (lasting exactly ten years). However, the words "but if" are words of limitation that create a term of years on executory limitation (subject to divestment). Asterix can lose possession of his term of years if he leaves the Gaelic resistance.

The words of purchase "to Idefix" denote Idefix as the grantee of a future interest. The words of limitation "and his heirs" identify the estate (that will exist if the future interest becomes possessory) as a fee simple. Since a future interest in a third party can divest the preceding estate, Idefix's interest is an executory interest. It is a shifting interest because Idefix, a transferee, will divest Asterix, another transferee, of the estate.

Since Obelix carved out a potentially smaller estate from his larger estate, he retains a future interest known as a reversion. Obelix's reversion will become possessory upon the expiration of the term of years if Asterix is not divested of the term of years by then.   If Asterix does leave the resistance, however, then Idefix's interest will become possessory (in fee simple), and Obelix's reversion will expire.

The executory interest does not violate the Rule Against Perpetuities. Asterix is a life in being at the creation of the interest. We know for certain that the condition (Asterix leaves the Gaelic resistance) will happen, if at all, during Asterix's lifetime (a life in being's lifetime). There is no possibility of remote vesting of the executory interest.

16.   Fitzgilbert ➜ Godwine for life, then to Oakes for life if he divorces his wife, then to
                       Godwine's heirs.

T	
SoT	

16.   Fitzgilbert ➜   Godwine for life, then to Oakes for life if he divorces his wife, then to
                        Godwine's heirs.

T	Fitzgilbert to Godwine in <u>life estate</u>, then to Oakes in <u>life estate</u> if he divorces his wife, then to Godwine's heirs in <u>fee simple</u>	
SoT	Godwine	- life estate
	Oakes	- contingent remainder in life estate
	Godwine's heirs	- contingent remainder in fee simple
	Fitzgilbert	- reversion

The rule in Shelley's Case applies. The interests should read:

M(SC)	Godwine	- life estate
	Oakes	- contingent remainder in life estate
	Godwine	- vested remainder in fee simple

The words of purchase "to Godwine" denote Godwine as the grantee of the present possessory interest; thus, he receives the estate. The words of limitation "for life" identify the estate as a life estate.

The words of purchase "to Oakes" denote Oakes as the grantee of a future interest. The words of limitation "for life" identify the estate (that will exist if the future interest becomes possessory) as a life estate. The interest is a remainder because (i) it is capable of becoming possessory immediately upon the expiration of the preceding estate and (ii) it cannot divest any other interests. It is a contingent remainder because it is subject to the condition precedent that Oakes divorce his wife.

The words of purchase "to Godwine's heirs" denote the grantee(s) of a future interest. There are no words of limitation, so a fee simple is presumed. The interest is a remainder because (i) it is capable of becoming possessory immediately upon the expiration of the preceding estate and (ii) it cannot divest any other interests. It is a contingent remainder because, at the time of the conveyance, Godwine's heirs are unascertainable [you cannot point to them].

Fitzgilbert retains a future interest known as a reversion. A reversion will always follow a contingent remainder because someone must hold seisin in the estate at all times. Since a contingent remainder is not certain to vest, the grantor must hold a reversion.

Shelley's Rule applies because there is one instrument creating a life estate in a transferee (Godwine), followed by a remainder in that transferee's (Godwine's) heirs, and both the life estate and the remainder are legal interests. The remainder in Godwine's heirs becomes a remainder in fee simple in Godwine. In effect, the words of purchase [Godwine's heirs] become words of limitation [Godwine and heirs]. It is vested because (i) Godwine is ascertainable [you can point to him] and (ii) there is no condition precedent.

17. Jarold ➔ Hans for ever and ever, until Hans marries Gertrude, then to Bertha.

T	
SoT	

17.   Jarold ➔ Hans for ever and ever, until Hans marries Gertrude, then to Bertha.

T	Jarold to Hans in <u>fee simple</u> until Hans marries Gertrude, then to Bertha in <u>fee simple</u>.
SoT	Hans - fee simple on executory limitation. Bertha - shifting executory interest

The words of purchase "to Hans" denote Hans as the grantee of the present possessory interest. Thus, he receives the estate. "For ever and ever" are not words of limitation, but they reflect Jarold's intent to give his entire interest, so modernly the interest is deemed to be a fee simple. However, the words of limitation "until" create a fee simple determinable, which is a defeasible fee. Since a third party, Bertha, will divest Hans of his estate, Hans has a fee simple on executory limitation. Hans will lose the estate if he ever marries Gertrude.

The words of purchase "to Bertha" denote Bertha as the grantee of a future interest. There are no words of limitation, so a fee simple is presumed. Bertha's interest is an executory interest because it will divest the preceding estate. It is a shifting interest because Bertha, a transferee, will divest Hans, another transferee, of the estate.

The executory interest does not violate the Rule Against Perpetuities. Hans is a life in being at the creation of the interest. We know for certain that the condition (Hans marries Gertrude) will happen, if at all, during a life in being's lifetime (Hans'). There is no possibility of remote vesting.

18.   Octavius ➔ Brutus and his heirs for as long as he continues to tend the yard, then to
        Octavius's heirs.

        Fact: Octavius is alive.

T	
SoT	

18.   Octavius ➡ Brutus and his heirs as long as he continues to tend the yard, then to
              Octavius's heirs.

Fact: Octavius is alive.

T	Octavius to Brutus in <u>fee simple</u> **as long as** he continues to tend the yard, then to Octavius's heirs in <u>fee simple</u>.
SoT	Brutus — fee simple on executory limitation Octavius's heirs — shifting executory interest in fee simple.

Doctrine of Worthier Title applies. The interests should read:

M(WT)	Brutus — fee simple determinable Octavius — possibility of reverter

The words of purchase "to Brutus" denote Brutus as the grantee of the present possessory interest; thus, he receives the estate. The words of limitation "and his heirs" identify the estate as a fee simple. However, the words "as long as" create a fee simple determinable, which is a defeasible fee. Since the defeasible fee is followed by a future interest in a third party, Brutus has a fee simple on executory limitation. His interest will be cut short if he fails to tend to the yard.

The words of purchase to "Octavius' heirs" denote the grantee(s) of a future interest. There are no words of limitation, so a fee simple is presumed. Since Octavius' heirs' future interest follows a defeasible fee, it is an executory interest. It is a shifting interest because Octavius' heirs, transferees, will divest Brutus, another transferee, of the estate. The interest of Octavius' heirs becomes possessory if, and when, Brutus fails to tend the yard.

The Doctrine of Worthier Title applies because the conveyance is inter vivos, and an executory interest is created in the grantor's (Octavius') heirs. Under the rule, the <u>presumption</u> is that no interest is created in Octavius's heirs; rather Octavius (the grantor) intends to retain a future interest in himself. In effect, the words of purchase ("to Octavius' heirs") become words of limitation ("to Octavius and heirs).

Thus, the state of title becomes: Brutus - fee simple determinable; Octavius - possibility of reverter.

19.   Oddvar ➔ Tahir for life, then to Tahir's first child to reach 30 and his heirs.

Fact: Tahir has a twenty year old son, Khalid.

T	
SoT	

19.   Oddvar ➔ Tahir for life, then to Tahir's first child to reach 30 and his heirs.

Fact: Tahir has a twenty year old son, Khalid.

T	Oddvar to Tahir in <u>life estate</u>, then to Tahir's first child to reach 30 in <u>fee simple</u>.
SoT	Tahir - life estate Tahir's 1st child ...30 - contingent remainder in fee simple Oddvar - reversion

Tahir's first child to reach 30's interest violates RAP. The interests should read:

M(RAP)	Tahir - life estate Oddvar - reversion.

The words of purchase "to Tahir" denote Tahir as the grantee of the present possessory interest; thus, he receives the estate. The words of limitation "for life" identify the estate as a life estate.

The words of purchase "to Tahir's first child to reach 30" denote the grantee of a future interest. The words of limitation "and his heirs" identify the estate (that will exist if the future interest becomes possessory) as a fee simple. The interest is a remainder because (i) it is capable of becoming possessory immediately upon the expiration of the preceding estate and (ii) it cannot divest any other interests. It is contingent because, at the time of the conveyance, the child is unascertainable [you cannot point to her]. If, and when, a child of Tahir's reaches 30, the remainder will vest.

Oddvar retains a future interest known as a reversion. A reversion will always follow a contingent remainder since someone must hold seisin in the estate at all times. Since a contingent remainder is not certain to vest, the grantor must retain a reversion.

Because the conveyance creates a contingent remainder, one must consider whether or not the interest violates RAP:

List the lives in being:

Tahir, Khalid and Oddvar are alive at the time of the conveyance. Therefore, they are the lives in being.

Give birth to any potential afterborns:

Tahir may have a child, Namish, after the conveyance. Namish is not a life in being for purposes of the Rule.

Kill off the lives in being and add 21 years:

Suppose that in 2010, Tahir, Khalid (who is then 25) and Oddvar all die. The lives in being are now dead. The "RAP line" becomes 2031.

Is there any possibility of remote vesting (that Namish can reach 30 after 2031)?

Is there any possibility that the contingent remainder may vest more than 21 years after all lives in being (Tahir, Khalid and Oddvar) die (past the 2031 "RAP line")? One possibility: A child of Tahir, Namish, is born in early 2010 (and therefore is not a life in being at creation). One day after the birth of Namish, Tahir, in his excitement over the news, slips in the snow, falls into Khalid and Oddvar, and the three of them meet an untimely end. The lives in being are now dead. Thirty years later (in 2040), Namish reaches 30, satisfying the condition precedent. His contingent remainder vests more than 21 years after the deaths of the lives in being, and RAP is violated.

When a conveyance violates the Rule Against Perpetuities, it does so when it is made, not 21 years later. The interest is void ab initio, from the moment that it is created. In the absence of reform tools, the offending interest is struck. Hence, the contingent remainder in Tahir's first child to reach 30 is blue-penciled out. The conveyance now reads:

Oddvar ➔ Tahir for life.

Tahir has a life estate. Oddvar has a reversion. Tahir's first child to reach 30 gets nothing.

Modern Applications:

If the conveyance violates the traditional Rule, look at it one more time. Check to see if you are in a jurisdiction that: (i) looks to see what actually happens during the perpetuities period applicable to the interest (Wait-and-See Doctrine); or (ii) permits reformation of the conveyance (Cy Pres Doctrine). If so, the conveyance may be saved.

Wait-and-See Jurisdiction: Wait until the end of the perpetuities period (lives in being plus 21 years). If, at this point in time the interest has vested, it is good. However, if it has not yet vested, the interest fails. Using this approach, we would wait 21 years after Tahir's death to see if one of his children has become 30. In this example, Namish would then only be 21, so his interest would fail. However, if the facts were slightly different and Tahir did not die until Namish was 15, then at the end of an additional 15 years Namish's interest would have vested. It would be good.

Cy Pres Jurisdiction: The court can rewrite the conveyance consistent with the grantor's general intentions. Utilizing Cy Pres, the conveyance might read:

Oddvar ➔ Tahir for life, then to Tahir's first child to reach 21.

20.   Henry ➔ Tabitha for life, then to Armond.

T	
SoT	

20.   Henry ➔ Tabitha for life, then to Armond.

T	Henry to Tabitha in <u>life estate</u>, then to Armond in <u>fee simple</u>.
SoT	Tabitha - life estate Armond - vested remainder in fee simple

The words of purchase "to Tabitha" denote Tabitha as the grantee of the present possessory interest; thus, she receives the estate. The words of limitation "for life" identify the estate as a life estate.

The words of purchase "to Armond" denote Armond as the grantee of a future interest. There are no words of limitation, so a fee simple is presumed. The interest is a remainder because (i) it is capable of becoming possessory immediately upon the expiration of the preceding estate and (ii) it cannot divest any other interests. It is vested because (i) Armond is ascertainable at the time of the conveyance [you can point to him] and (ii) there is no condition precedent. Armond will take the estate in fee simple upon the expiration of Tabitha's life estate.

Henry retains no interest because he has given away his entire fee simple.

21.   Groucho ➜ Harpo's heirs.

Fact: Harpo is alive.

T	
SoT	

21.   Groucho ➔ Harpo's heirs.

Fact: Harpo is alive.

T	Groucho to Harpo's heirs in <u>fee simple</u>	
SoT	Groucho Harpo's heirs	- fee simple on executory limitation - springing executory interest in fee simple

The words of purchase "to Harpo's heirs" denote Harpo's heirs as the grantees; thus, they would receive the estate. There are no words of limitation, so a fee simple is presumed.

Harpo's heirs are unascertainable at the time of conveyance; thus, Groucho retains possession until Harpo's death. [A person cannot have heirs until they die, only heirs apparent.] Harpo's heirs have a springing executory interest because the heirs, transferees, will divest Groucho, the transferor, of the estate.

Note, the Doctrine of Worthier Title does not apply as the grant is to a transferee's (Harpo's) heirs, rather than the grantor's (Groucho's) heirs.

22. Caelan ➜ Harvey and the heirs of his body by Sally.

T	
SoT	

22.   Caelan ➜ Harvey and the heirs of his body by Sally.

T	Caelan to Harvey in <u>fee tail special</u>.
SoT	Harvey - fee tail special Caelan - reversion

The words of purchase "to Harvey" denote Harvey as the grantee of the present possessory interest; thus, he receives the estate. The words of limitation "and the heirs of his body" identify the estate as a fee tail, in those jurisdictions that recognize the estate. The words "by Sally" place a particular condition on who may gain a possessory interest in the estate, creating a fee tail special.

Since Caelan carved out a smaller estate from her larger estate, she retains a future interest known as a reversion. Caelan's interest becomes possessory once the issue line of Harvey and Sally ceases.

23.   Igor ➔ Cadence for life, then to Matilda for life, then to Cadence's heirs.

T	
SoT	

23. Igor ➜ Cadence for life, then to Matilda for life, then to Cadence's heirs.

T	Igor to Cadence in <u>life estate</u>, then to Matilda in <u>life estate</u>, then to Cadence's heirs in <u>fee simple</u>.	
SoT	Cadence Matilda Cadence's heirs Igor	- life estate - vested remainder in life estate - contingent remainder in fee simple – reversion

The Rule in Shelley's Case applies. The interests should read:

M (SC)	Cadence Matilda Cadence	– life estate – vested remainder in life estate – vested remainder in fee simple

The words of purchase "to Cadence" denote Cadence as the grantee of the present possessory interest; thus, she receives the estate. The words of limitation "for life" identify the estate as a life estate.

The words of purchase "to Matilda" denote Matilda as the grantee of a future interest. The words of limitation "for life" identify the estate (that will exist if the future interest becomes possessory) as a life estate. The interest is a remainder because (i) it is capable of becoming possessory immediately upon the expiration of the preceding estate and (ii) it cannot divest any other interests. It is vested because (i) Matilda is ascertainable at the time of the conveyance [you can point to her] and there is no condition precedent.

The words of purchase "to Cadence's heirs" denote the grantee(s) of a future interest. There are no words of limitation, so a fee simple is presumed. The interest is a remainder because (i) it is capable of becoming possessory immediately upon the expiration of the preceding estate and (ii) it cannot divest any other interests. It is a contingent remainder because, at the time of the conveyance, Cadence's heirs are unascertainable [you cannot point to them].

Igor retains a future interest known as a reversion. A reversion will always follow a contingent remainder because someone must hold seisin in the estate at all times. Since a contingent remainder is not certain to vest, the grantor must retain a reversion.

Shelley's Rule applies because there is one instrument, creating a life estate in a transferee (Cadence), followed by a remainder in that transferee's (Cadence's) heirs, and both the life estate and the remainder are legal interests. The remainder in Cadence's heirs becomes a remainder in fee simple in Cadence. In effect, the words of purchase [Cadence's heirs] become words of limitation [Cadence and heirs]. It is vested because (i) Cadence is ascertainable [you can point to him] and (ii) there is no condition precedent.

Cadence's vested remainder in fee simple follows Matilda's vested remainder in life estate. [Cadence's heirs or devisees will likely take possession at the end of Matilda's life estate.]

24.   Bernie ➔ Zebulon for ten years, then to Zebulon's heirs.

T	
SoT	

24.   Bernie ➔ Zebulon for ten years, then to Zebulon's heirs.

T	Bernie to Zebulon for <u>a term of years</u>, then to Zebulon's heirs in <u>fee simple</u>.
SoT	Zebulon - term of years Zebulon's heirs - springing executory interest in fee simple Bernie - reversion

The words of purchase "to Zebulon" denote Zebulon as the grantee of the present possessory interest; thus he receives the estate. The words of limitation "for ten years" identify the estate as a term of years, which is a leasehold estate of fixed duration (here, lasting exactly 10 years).

The words of purchase "to Zebulon's heirs" denote the grantee(s) of a future interest. There are no words of limitation, so a fee simple is presumed. Zebulon's heirs' future interest is not a remainder because a contingent remainder may never follow a term of years. Therefore, an executory interest is created. It is a springing interest because Zebulon's heirs, transferees, will divest Bernie, the transferor, of the estate.

Bernie retains a future interest known as a reversion. A reversion will always follow a term of years because someone must hold seisin in the estate at all times. Since a term of years is a leasehold estate, the grantor must retain a reversion.

Shelley's Rule does not apply because the interest transferred was a leasehold (a non-freehold estate), and not a freehold estate.

25.   Michael ➜ Roman for life, then to Peter for life, then to Peter's heirs.

T	
SoT	

25.   Michael ➔ Roman for life, then to Peter for life, then to Peter's heirs.

T	Michael to Roman in <u>life estate</u>, then to Peter in <u>life estate</u>, then to Peter's heirs in <u>fee simple</u>.
SoT	Roman — life estate Peter — vested remainder in life estate Peter's heirs — contingent remainder in fee simple Michael — reversion

The Rule in Shelley's Case applies. The interests should read:

M (SC)	Roman — life estate Peter — vested remainder in fee simple

The words of purchase "to Roman" denote Roman as the grantee of the present possessory interest; thus, he receives the estate. The words of limitation "for life" identify the estate as a life estate.

The words of purchase "to Peter" denote Peter as the grantee of a future interest. The words of limitation "for life" identify the estate (that will exist if the future interest becomes possessory) as a life estate. The interest is a remainder because (i) it is capable of becoming possessory immediately upon the expiration of the preceding estate and (ii) it cannot divest any other interests. It is vested because (i) Peter is ascertainable [you can point to him] and (ii) there is no condition precedent.

The words of purchase "to Peter's heirs" denote the grantee(s) of a future interest. There are no words of limitation, so a fee simple is presumed. The interest is a remainder because (i) it is capable of becoming possessory immediately upon the expiration of the preceding estate and (ii) it cannot divest any other interests. It is a contingent remainder because, at the time of the conveyance, Peter's heirs are unascertainable [you cannot point to them].

Michael retains a future interest known as a reversion. A reversion will always follow a contingent remainder because someone must hold seisin in the estate at all times. Since a contingent remainder is not certain to vest, the grantor must retain a reversion.

Shelley's Rule applies because there is one instrument creating a life estate in a transferee (Peter), followed by a remainder in that transferee's (Peter's) heirs, and both the life estate and the remainder are legal interests. It is not necessary that the life estate be present possessory; it may exist as a future interest.

The Doctrine of Merger would apply in this situation, merging Peter's remainder in life estate and Peter's remainder in fee simple. The state of the title now reads:

M (SC)	Roman — life estate Peter — vested remainder in fee simple

26.　　　　Herb ➔ Brenda for life, then to Juliette if she becomes an attorney.

T	
SoT	

26.   Herb ➔ Brenda for life, then to Juliette if she becomes an attorney.

T	Herb to Brenda in <u>life estate</u>, then to Juliette in <u>fee simple </u>if she becomes an attorney.
SoT	Brenda - life estate Juliette - contingent remainder in fee simple Herb - reversion

The words of purchase "to Brenda" denote Brenda as the grantee of the present possessory interest; thus, she receives the estate. The words of limitation "for life" identify the estate as a life estate.

The words of purchase "to Juliette" denote Juliette as the grantee of a future interest. There are no words of limitation so a fee simple is presumed. The interest is a remainder because (i) it is capable of becoming possessory immediately upon the expiration of the preceding estate and (ii) it cannot divest any other interests. It is a contingent remainder because it is subject to the condition precedent that Juliette become an attorney.

Herb retains a future interest known as a reversion. A reversion will always follow a contingent remainder because someone must hold seisin in the estate at all times. Since a contingent remainder is not certain to vest, the grantor must retain a reversion.

The contingent remainder does not violate the Rule Against Perpetuities. Juliette is a life in being at the creation of the interest. We know for certain that the condition (Juliette becomes an attorney) will happen, if at all, during a life in being's lifetime (Juliette's). There is no possibility of remote vesting.

In a jurisdiction that applies the Doctrine of Destructibility of Contingent Remainders -- if Juliette is not an attorney when Brenda dies, her contingent remainder is "destroyed," and she loses any and all interest in the estate. Herb's reversion would then become possessory.

In a non-destructibility jurisdiction -- if Juliette is not an attorney when Brenda dies, then the estate would revert to the grantor, Herb, to hold in fee simple on executory limitation until the condition is satisfied, or until it is no longer capable of being performed (Juliette's death). Juliette would hold an executory interest.

27.   Alim ➔ Florimel and her heirs to be used as an antique store.

T	
SoT	

27.   Alim ➜ Florimel and her heirs to be used as an antique store.

T	Florimel in <u>fee simple</u> to be used as an antique store.
SoT	Florimel - fee simple

The words of purchase "to Florimel" denote Florimel as the grantee of the present possessory interest; thus, she receives the estate. The words of limitation "and her heirs" identify the estate as a fee simple. Words of divestment are not present in the conveyance; therefore, given the modern presumption in favor of a fee simple, the words [to be used as an antique store] would likely be construed to be the rationale or motive for the conveyance, rather than a limitation on the estate.

The grantor retains no future interest because there are no words indicating that the estate be a defeasible fee. Alim does not have the power to gain possession of the premises if the estate is not used as an antique store. Florimel has a fee simple absolute.

28.   Starkadhr ➔   Fisk for life, then to Tobias for life if he buys a white stallion, then to
Fisk's heirs.

T	
SoT	

28.   Starkadhr ➜   Fisk for life, then to Tobias for life if he buys a white stallion, then to
                       Fisk's heirs.

T	Starkadhr to Fisk in <u>life estate</u>, then to Tobias in <u>life estate</u> if he buys a white stallion, then to Fisk's heirs in <u>fee simple</u>.	
SoT	Fisk	- life estate
	Tobias	- contingent remainder in life estate
	Fisk's heirs	- contingent remainder in fee simple
	Starkadhr	- vested remainder in fee simple

M(SC)	Fisk	– life estate
	Tobias	– contingent remainder in life estate
	Fisk	– vested remainder in fee simple

Initial Parsing:

The words of purchase "to Fisk" denote Fisk as the grantee of the present possessory interest; thus, he receives the estate. The words of limitation "for life" identify the estate as a life estate.

The words of purchase "to Tobias" denote Tobias as the grantee of a future interest. The words of limitation "for life" identify the estate (that will exist if the future interest becomes possessory) as a life estate. The interest is a remainder because (i) it is capable of becoming possessory immediately upon the expiration of the preceding estate and (ii) it cannot divest any other interests. It is a contingent remainder because it is subject to the condition precedent that Tobias buy a white stallion.

The words of purchase "to Fisk's heirs" denote Fisk's heirs as the grantee(s) of a future interest. There are no words of limitation, so a fee simple is presumed. The interest is a remainder because (i) it is capable of becoming possessory immediately upon the expiration of the preceding estate and (ii) it cannot divest any other interests. It is a contingent remainder because Fisk's heirs are unascertainable [you cannot point to them].

Starkadhr retains a future interest known as a reversion. A reversion will always follow a contingent remainder because someone must hold seisin in the estate at all times. Since a contingent remainder is not certain to vest, the grantor must retain a reversion.

Shelley's Rule applies because there is one instrument creating a life estate in a transferee (Fisk), followed by a remainder in that transferee's (Fisk's) heirs, and both the life estate and the remainder are legal interests. The remainder in Fisk's heirs becomes a remainder in fee simple in Fisk. In effect, the words of purchase ("Fisk's heirs") become words of limitation ("Fisk and heirs"). Fisk has a vested remainder in fee simple.

29.   Honigmann ➔ Strack for ever and ever.

T	
SoT	

29.   Honigmann ➔ Strack for ever and ever.

T	Honigmann to Strack in <u>fee simple</u>.
SoT	Strack - fee simple

The words of purchase "to Strack" denote Strack as the grantee of the present possessory interest; thus, he receives the estate. The words "for ever and ever" are not words of limitation, but they reflect Honigmann's intent to give his entire interest to Strack. If the conveyance does not contain traditional words of limitation, it is presumed that the grantor conveyed the largest possible estate, a fee simple.

30.   Joaquin ➜ Addison for 59 years.

T	
SoT	

30.   Joaquin ➜ Addison for 59 years.

T	Joaquin to Addison for <u>a term of years</u>.
SoT	Addison - term of years Joaquin - reversion

The words of purchase "to Addison" denote Addison as the grantee of the present possessory interest; thus he receives the estate. The words of limitation "for 59 years" identify the estate as a term of years. A term of years is an estate of fixed duration, in this case lasting exactly 59 years.

Since Joaquin did not convey his entire interest, he retains a reversion.

VI. Summary Charts

Present Possessory Estates

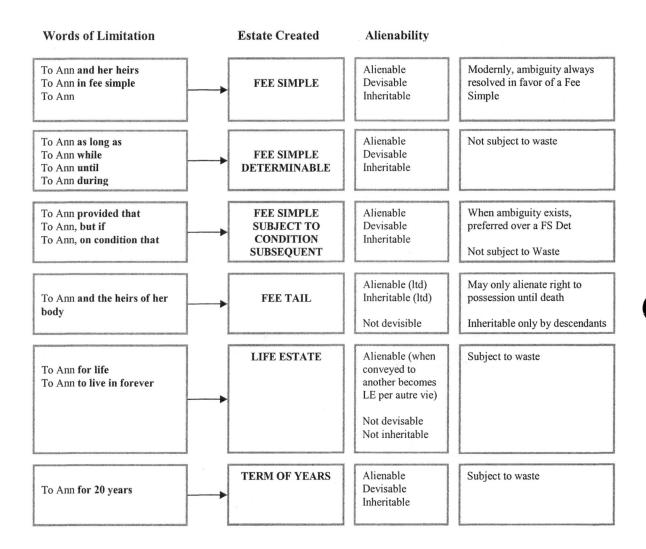

Words of Limitation	Estate Created	Alienability	
To Ann **and her heirs** To Ann **in fee simple** To Ann	**FEE SIMPLE**	Alienable Devisable Inheritable	Modernly, ambiguity always resolved in favor of a Fee Simple
To Ann **as long as** To Ann **while** To Ann **until** To Ann **during**	**FEE SIMPLE DETERMINABLE**	Alienable Devisable Inheritable	Not subject to waste
To Ann **provided that** To Ann, **but if** To Ann, **on condition that**	**FEE SIMPLE SUBJECT TO CONDITION SUBSEQUENT**	Alienable Devisable Inheritable	When ambiguity exists, preferred over a FS Det Not subject to Waste
To Ann **and the heirs of her body**	**FEE TAIL**	Alienable (ltd) Inheritable (ltd) Not devisible	May only alienate right to possession until death Inheritable only by descendants
To Ann **for life** To Ann **to live in forever**	**LIFE ESTATE**	Alienable (when conveyed to another becomes LE per autre vie) Not devisable Not inheritable	Subject to waste
To Ann **for 20 years**	**TERM OF YEARS**	Alienable Devisable Inheritable	Subject to waste

Future Interests

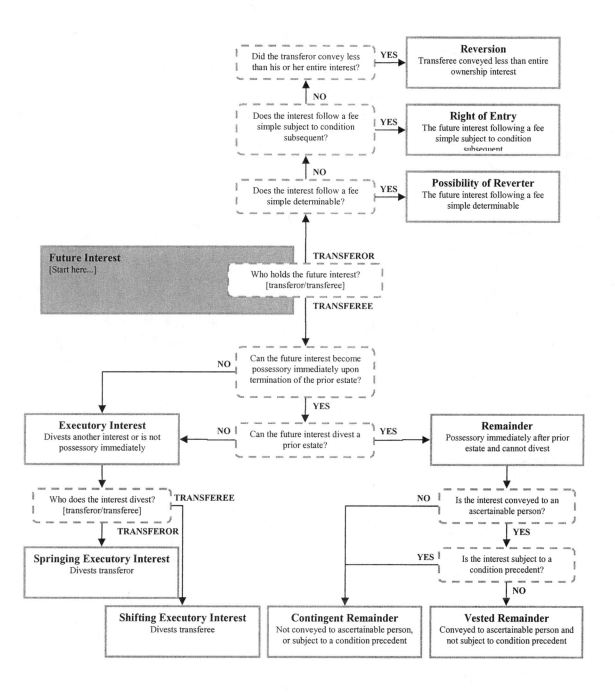

Rules Furthering Marketability

Rule in Shelley's Case

Where a single instrument creates a freehold estate in a transferee, and a remainder in the transferee's heirs, this rule operates to transfer that remainder to the transferee.

- Operative at the time of conveyance.
- Applies only to remainders--not executory interests. Usually, this rule is applied to conveyances involving an interest following a life estate.
- In this rule, the two interests are in the transferee and transferee's heirs.
- The two interests must be created by the same instrument.
- The interests must both be legal or both be equitable (i.e., a trust).
- This rule is a rule of law and ignores the intent of the grantor.

Doctrine of Worthier Title

If a grantor creates a future interest in his or her own heirs, that future interests is converted to a reversion (an interest in the grantor).

- Operative at the time of conveyance.
- Applies to both contingent remainders and executory interests.
- In this rule, the compatible interests are in the grantor and grantor's heirs.
- This rule is a rule of construction. It does not override the clearly expressed intent of the grantor.

Destructibility of Contingent Remainders

A contingent remainder is destroyed if it has not vested at the termination of the prior estate.

- Operative at the termination of the prior estate.
- This rule is a rule of law and ignores the intent of the grantor.

Rule Against Perpetuities

If there is any possibility of an interest vesting (in interest) after the expiration of the perpetuities period, that interest is stricken from the original conveyance.

- The rule against perpetuities is operative at the time of conveyance.
- The rule against perpetuities applies to all of the following: contingent remainders, executory interests, and vested remainders subject to open.
- All future interests in the grantor are considered vested for the purposes of this rule.
- The traditional perpetuities period is twenty one (21) years from the death of the last life in being.
- Lives in being are determined at the time of conveyance. In the case of a conveyance by will, the lives in being are determined at the time of the grantor's death.
- This rule is a rule of law and ignores the intent of the grantor.
- After applying the traditional rule against perpetuities, consider modern applications (wait and see, uniform statutory rule against perpetuities, and cy pres).